Grades
K-2

SLIDE INTO PHONICS

Alphabet & Letter Sounds

Super-Fun Reproducible Activity Pages and Hands-On Learning Tools

Develops Foundational Reading Skills!

MICHELLE STURM

SCHOLASTIC

Publisher: Tara Welty
Editor: Lynne M. Wilson
Cover design: Tannaz Fassihi and Cynthia Ng
Interior design: Jaime Lucero
Interior illustrations: Rob McClurkan, Doug Jones, Noun Project

ISBN 978-1-5461-5260-6

Scholastic Inc., 557 Broadway, New York, NY 10012
Copyright © 2025 Scholastic Inc.
All rights reserved. Made in U.S.A.
First printing, January 2025

1 2 3 4 5 6 7 8 9 10   40   34 33 32 31 30 29 28 27 26 25

Table of Contents

Welcome to *Slide Into Phonics: Alphabet & Letter Sounds*!

This book offers a diverse range of activities that blend phonics practice with research-based, hands-on approaches. From engaging slider manipulatives and writing practice to fun picture puzzles, each activity builds alphabet knowledge and letter-sound correspondence, strengthens fine-motor skills, and instills a love of learning. These bite-sized activities were designed to fit your busy schedule, ensuring they are easy to implement while providing beneficial instruction. The result? A strong phonics foundation for reading success!

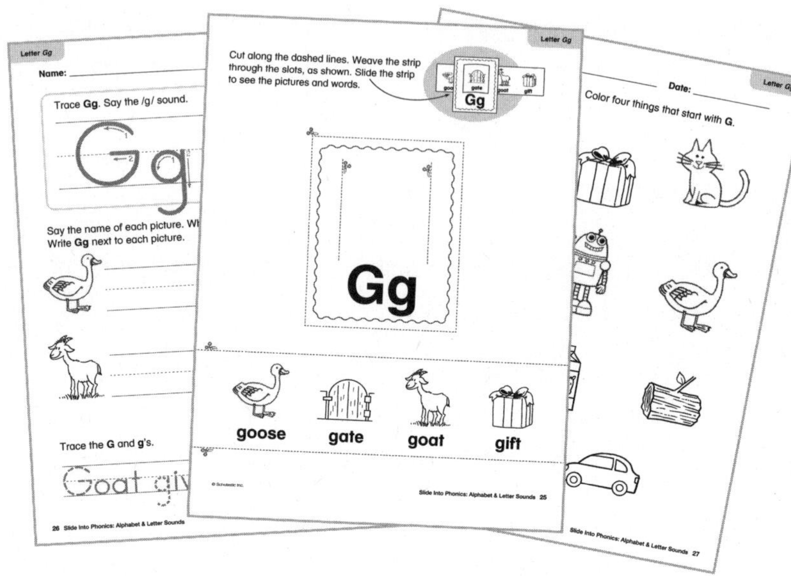

Research shows that one of the predictors of early reading success is alphabet recognition—knowing the names of the letters, their shapes, and the sounds they represent.[1] Since identifying letters and their sounds is the starting block for learning to read, each reproducible page not only introduces each letter, but also focuses on the initial letter sound of common words. This book presents three activities for each letter of the alphabet:

Phonics Sliders—The star in every letter set is the slider manipulative. These sliders are fun and tangible tools that help children understand the relationship between letters and sounds. Research shows that hands-on learning allows children to explore abstract concepts, such as letter sounds, more concretely.[2] Once kids know the names of the letters of the alphabet, they are ready to connect the letters with words.

By sliding the letter and picture strips, early readers can discover the relationship between letters and sounds. To begin, model how to use the slider, emphasizing how to name the pictures and say their initial letter sound. For example, you might say: "*A* is for *apple. Apple* starts with the letter *A*. What sound do you hear at the beginning of apple?" As kids slide each picture into the frame, invite them to point to the image, name it, and then say the initial letter sound. Then, they can point to the word and read it aloud.

Writing Practice Pages—Each set of activities includes a dedicated exercise designed to enhance children's handwriting skills. By forming the shapes of the letters that represent each sound, children boost their phonemic-awareness, letter-sound correlation, and fine-motor skills. Research shows that writing by hand not only teaches letter formation but also strengthens language acquisition, neurological development, and reading fluency.[3] When introducing the activity, model saying the sound of each letter as you trace it, then ask children to say the sound with you, noticing the shape of your mouth. Encourage children to say the sound as they form each letter to reinforce letter-sound connection.

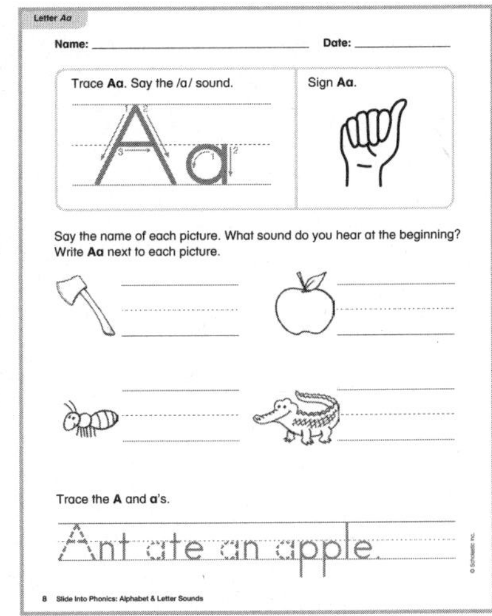

Each writing page also includes the American Sign Language hand sign for the letter. Learning sign language can boost cultural awareness in children and provide a multisensory approach to language development. Model how to sign the letter as you say its name. Help children sign the letter as needed. When children have learned all the letter signs, encourage them to use the sign for each letter as they sing the alphabet song. Connecting visual symbols and fine motor movement to specific sounds helps activate learning.[4]

Picture Finds—The third activity is a picture find that uses the same illustrations as those on the previous page, creating a cohesive and engaging learning experience. Have children say the name of each illustration, encouraging them to listen for the target initial letter sound—a great way to enhance both phonemic-awareness and visual-discrimination skills.

Bonus: Letter Flash Cards—At the back of this book, you'll also find a set of reproducible flash cards and suggested flash card games to further enrich children's learning experience and reinforce their phonics skills. You can copy the cards for each child to take home, use them in a learning center for partner review, or lead the class in playing one of the games together.

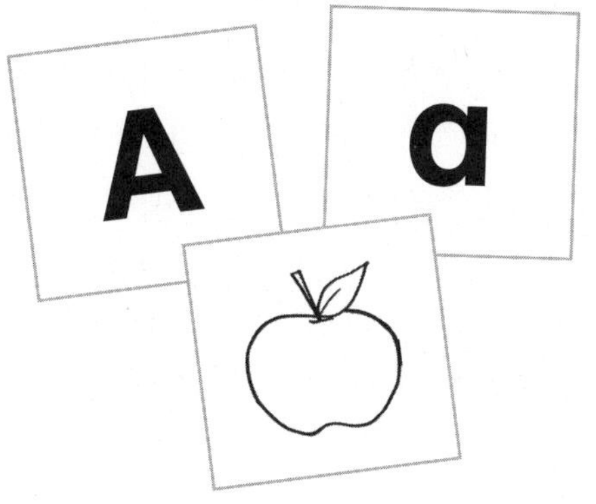

How to Use This Book

It is best to implement these reproducible activities after first introducing the respective letter and its sound. To weave each phonics activity into your busy schedule, consider offering one page per day or per week.

The phonics slider, for example, is a great follow-up to your lesson about a particular letter. Distribute copies of the slider page to children, along with scissors and crayons. Invite them to color the pictures before cutting the page apart. Some children may need help cutting out the windows on the sliders.

As children learn each letter, consider putting copies of the corresponding activity pages in your learning center for kids to explore and work on independently. You can also assign some activities, such as the writing practice or the picture search, as homework to maximize classroom time. Use these pages to informally assess children's knowledge and growth.

Slide Into Phonics: Alphabet & Letter Sounds is designed to supplement reading lessons via a unique blend of hands-on tools, writing exercises, visual aids, and interactive practice. We aim to enhance your lessons and motivate and excite children as they learn to read. Enjoy!

A NOTE ABOUT TEACHING SEQUENCE

In what order should you teach the letters? It's really up to you. The most popular approach is *A*-to-*Z* order because most kids arrive at school already knowing the alphabet song, which follows this sequence. Some educators, however, believe in teaching the highest-utility letters—those that appear most frequently in words— first, like *m, a, t, s, p, h.* They say this enables children to decode a large number of words in the early stages of reading instruction. Still others prefer to begin with *a, e, i, o,* and *u* to highlight the difference between vowels and consonants. At present, there is no clear evidence to indicate which approach works best. So, you may want to consider which of these three options aligns closest to your existing curriculum.

[1] McNeill, B. C., Gillon, G., & Gath, M. (2023). The relationship between early spelling and decoding. *Language, Speech, and Hearing Services in Schools, 54*(3), 981–995.

[2] Eggen, P. D., & Kauchak, D. P. (2024). *Using educational psychology in teaching.* Pearson.

[3] Gentry, J. R. (2023, September 15). *5 reasons why writing helps early reading.* Retrieved from https://www.psychologytoday.com/us/blog/raising-readers-writers-and-spellers/201309/5-reasons-why-writing-helps-early-reading

[4] Gejl, A. K., Malling, A. S., Damsgaard, L., Veber-Nielsen, A. -M., & Wienecke, J. (2021). Motor-enriched learning for improving pre-reading and word recognition skills in preschool children aged 5–6 years — study protocol for the playmore randomized controlled trial. *BMC Pediatrics, 21*(1).

Cut along the dashed lines. Weave the strip through the slots, as shown. Slide the strip to see the pictures and words.

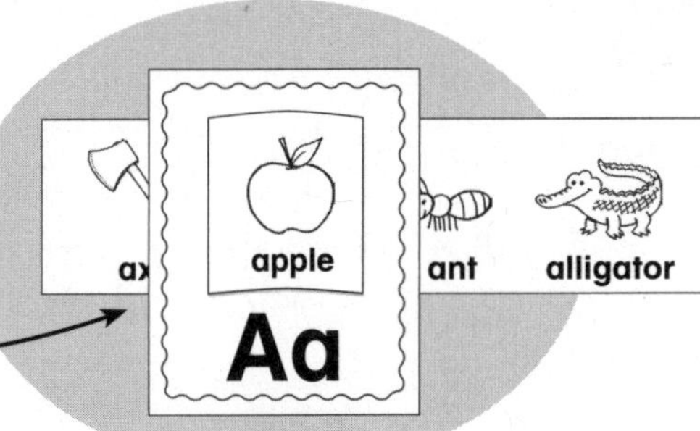

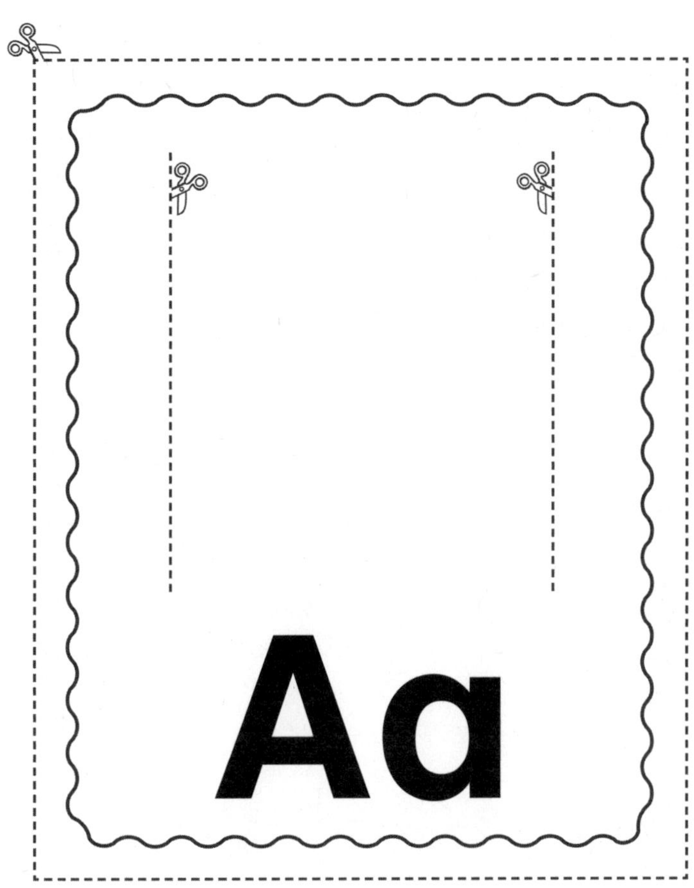

ax

apple

ant

alligator

Name: ___________________________   **Date:** ___________________

Trace Aa. Say the /a/ sound.

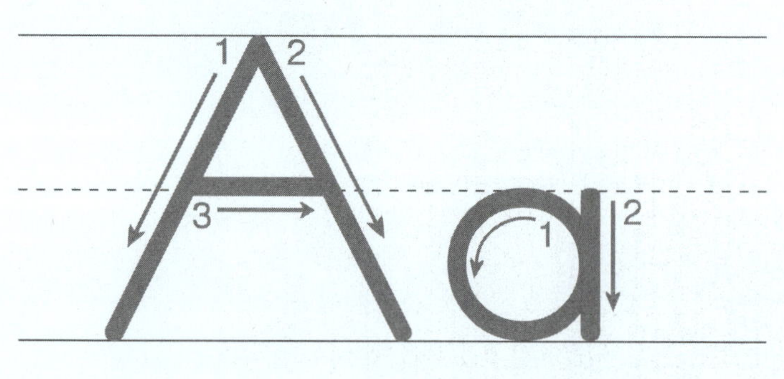

Sign Aa.

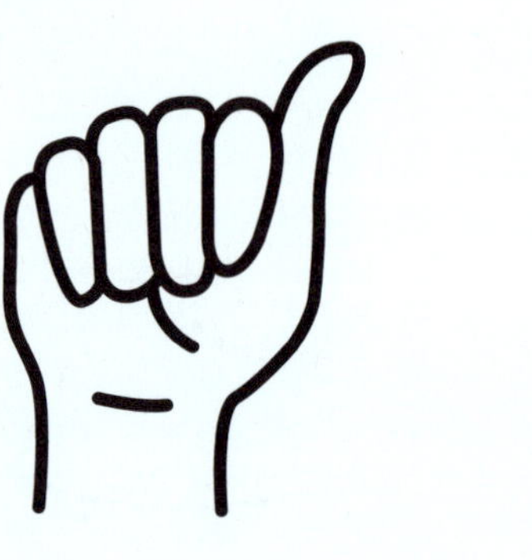

Say the name of each picture. What sound do you hear at the beginning? Write **Aa** next to each picture.

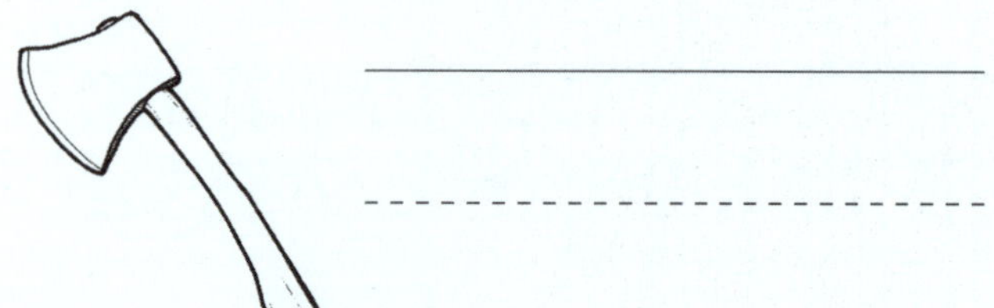

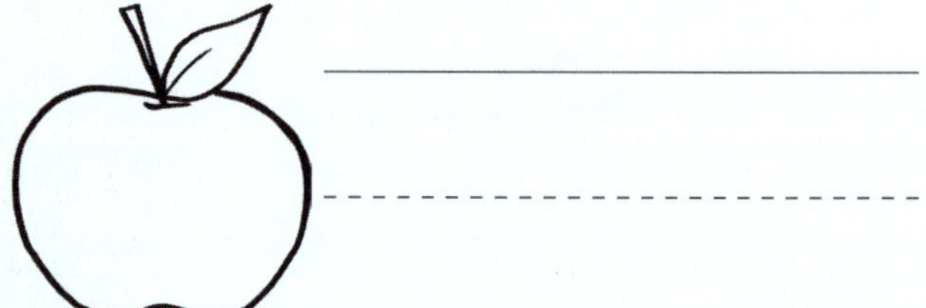

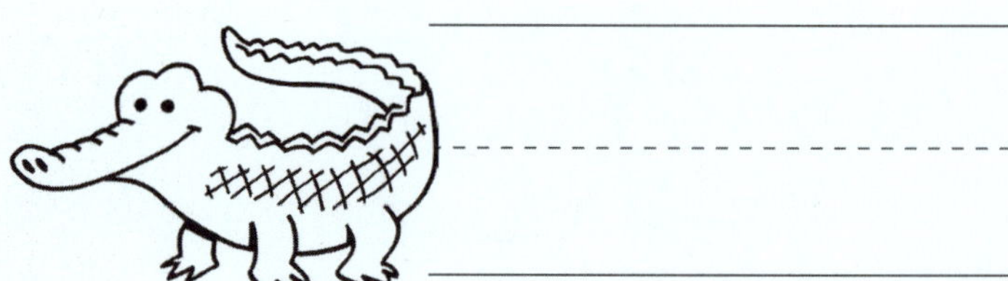

Trace the **A** and **a**'s.

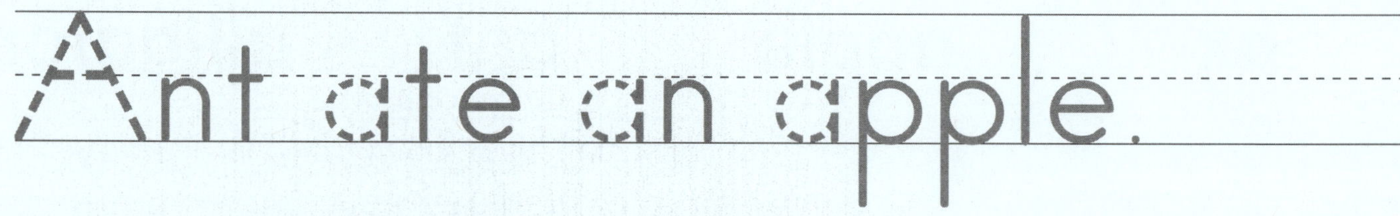

Name: _______________________   **Date:** _______________________

Say the name of each picture. Color four things that start with **A**.

Cut along the dashed lines. Weave the strip through the slots, as shown. Slide the strip to see the pictures and words.

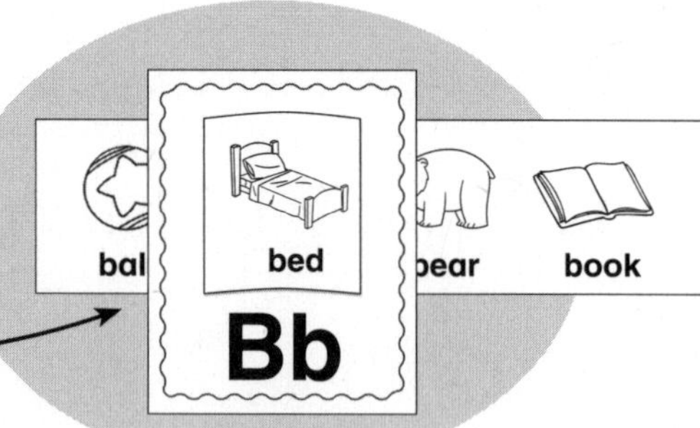

ball

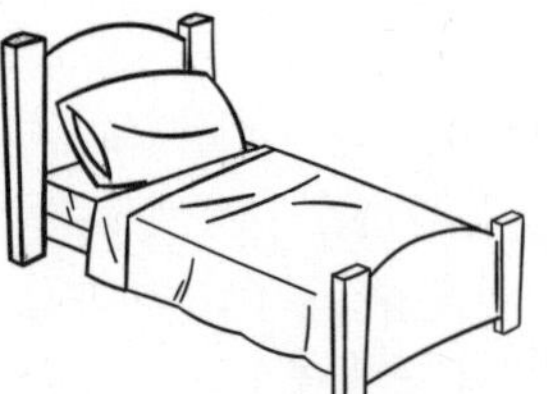

bed

bear

book

Name: ___________________________   **Date:** ___________________

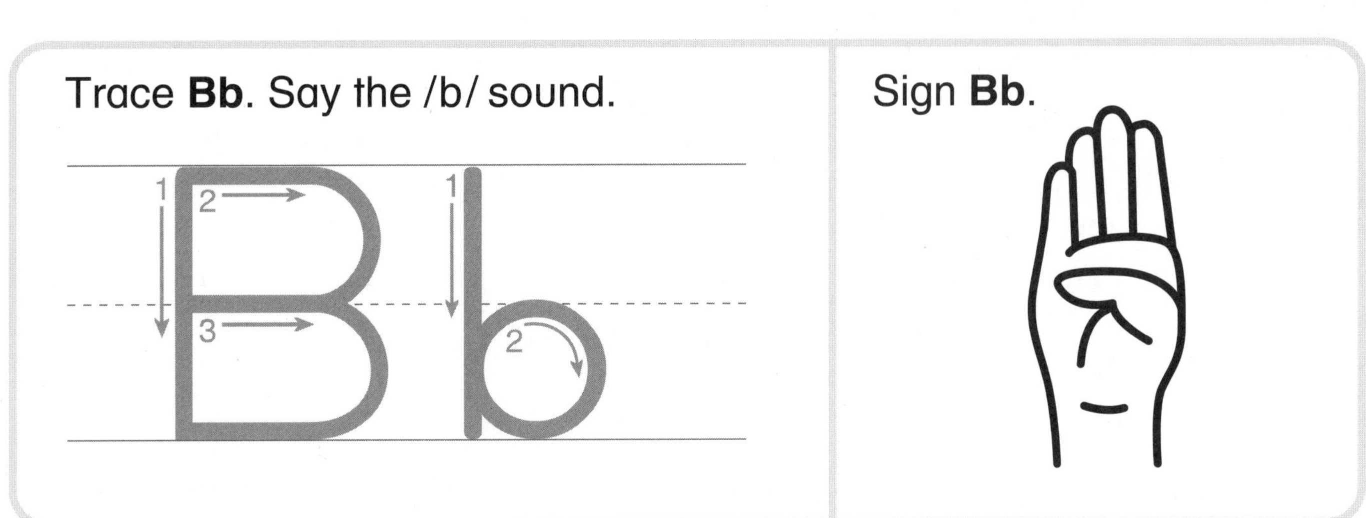

Say the name of each picture. What sound do you hear at the beginning? Write **Bb** next to each picture.

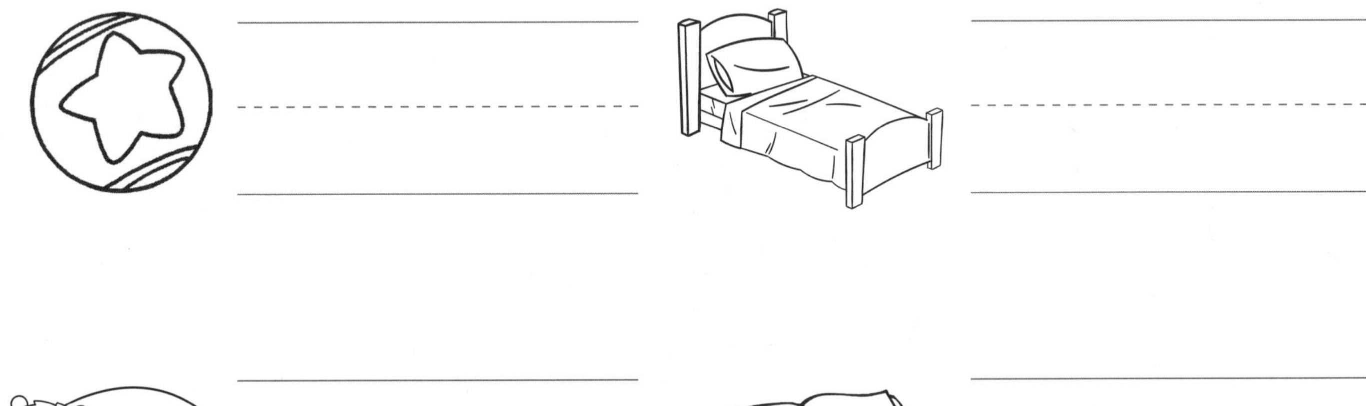

Trace the **B** and **b**'s.

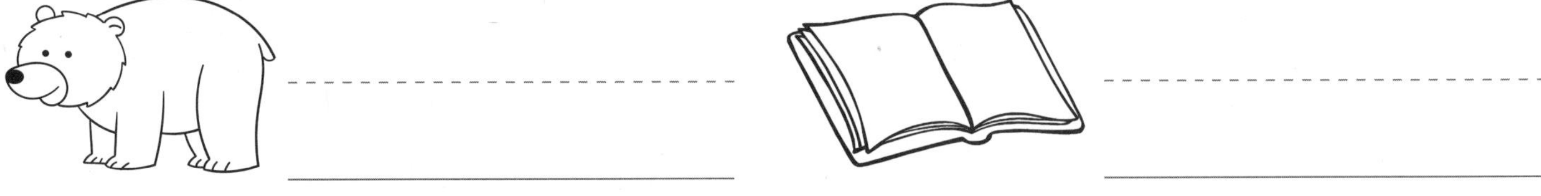

Name: _______________________________ **Date:** _______________

Say the name of each picture. Color four things that start with **B**.

Cut along the dashed lines. Weave the strip through the slots, as shown. Slide the strip to see the pictures and words.

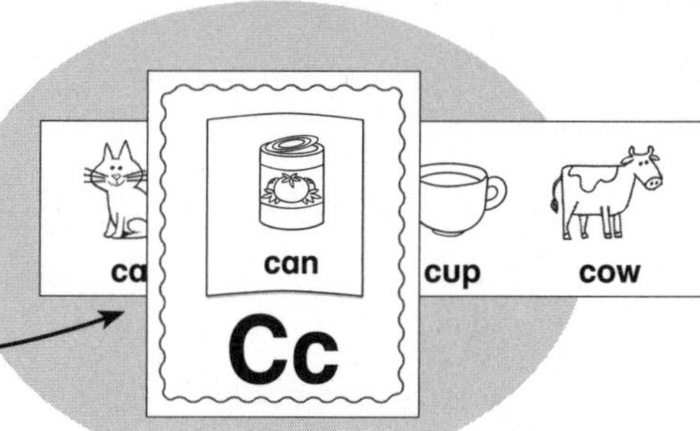

cat   **can**   **cup**   **cow**

Name: _______________________________   **Date:** _______________

Trace **Cc**. Say the /k/ sound.

Sign **Cc**.

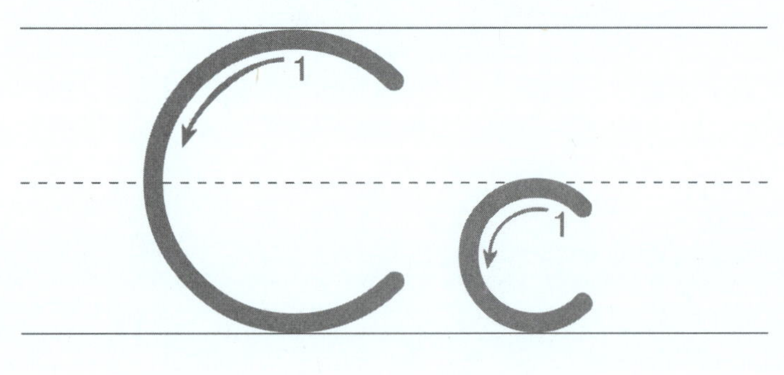

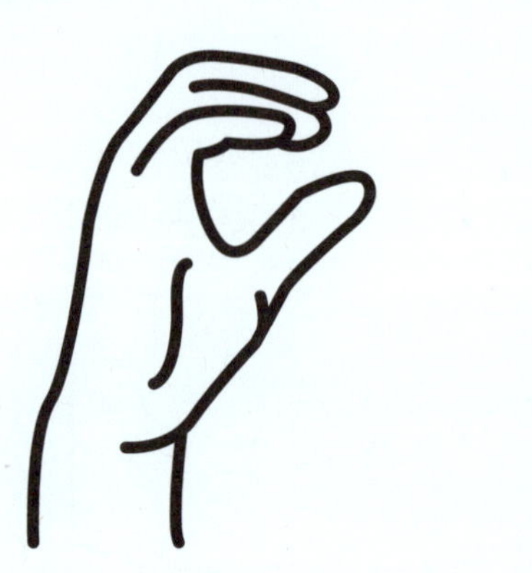

Say the name of each picture. What sound do you hear at the beginning? Write **Cc** next to each picture.

Trace the **C** and **c**'s.

Cat counts cans.

Name: ___________________________ **Date:** _______________

Say the name of each picture. Color four things that start with **C**.

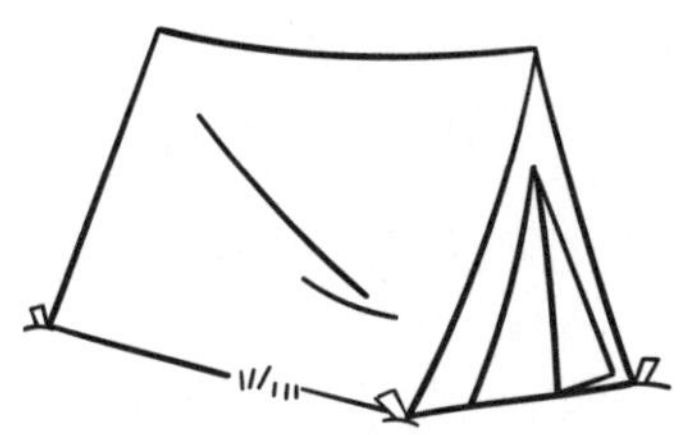  

Cut along the dashed lines. Weave the strip through the slots, as shown. Slide the strip to see the pictures and words.

dog

doll

duck

door

Name: _______________________ **Date:** _______________

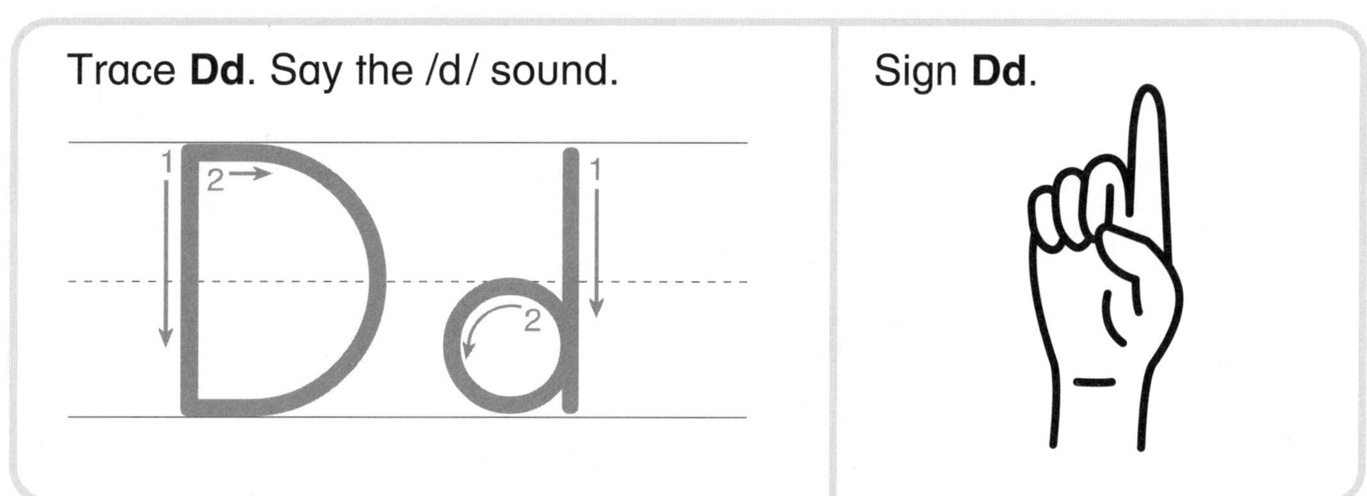

Trace **Dd**. Say the /d/ sound.

Sign **Dd**.

Say the name of each picture. What sound do you hear at the beginning?
Write **Dd** next to each picture.

Trace the **D**'s and **d**'s.

Name: _______________________________   **Date:** _______________

Say the name of each picture. Color four things that start with **D**.

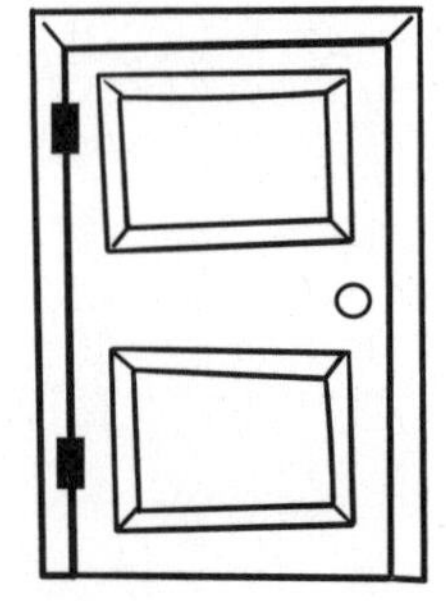

Cut along the dashed lines. Weave the strip through the slots, as shown. Slide the strip to see the pictures and words.

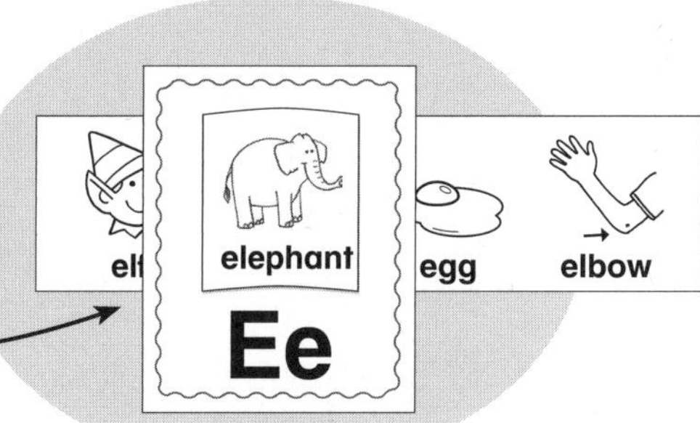

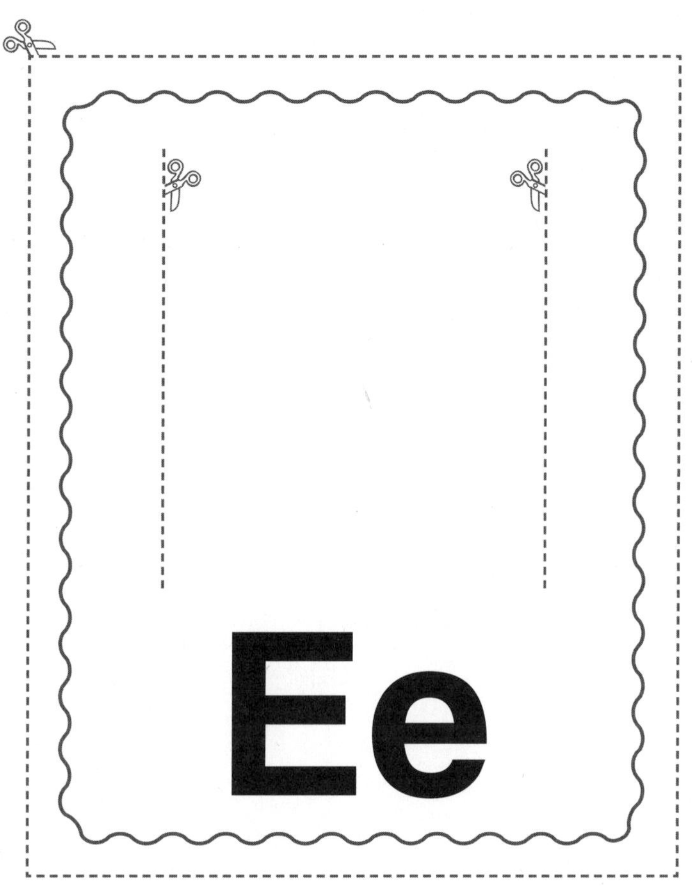

elf

elephant

egg

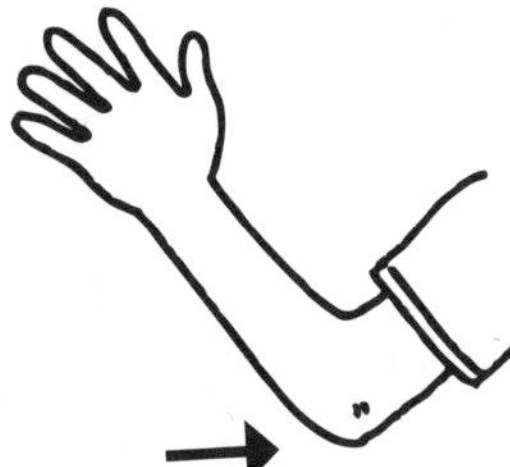

elbow

Name: _______________________________   **Date:** _______________

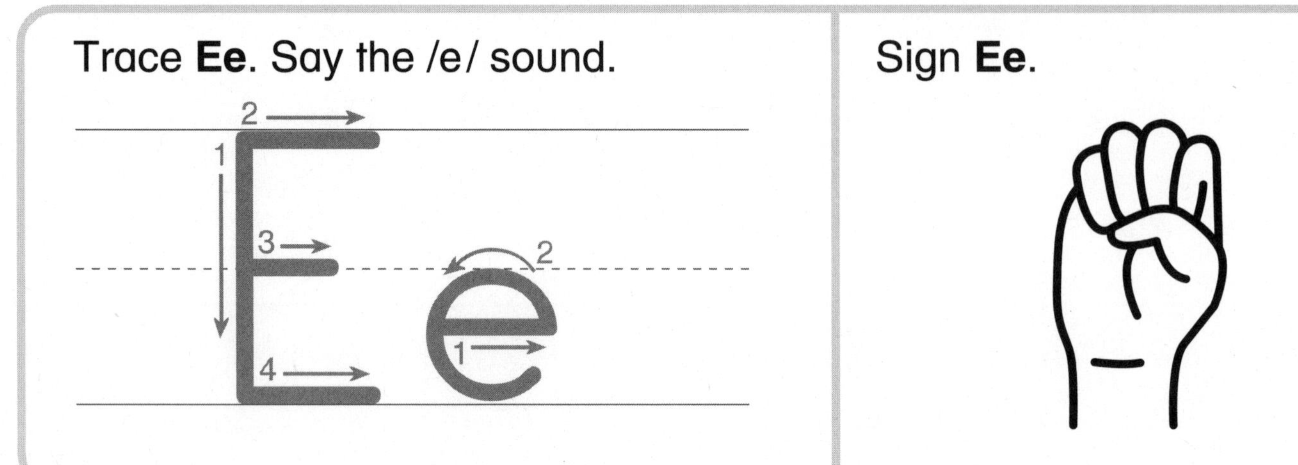

Say the name of each picture. What sound do you hear at the beginning? Write **Ee** next to each picture.

Trace the **E** and **e**'s.

Name: _______________________________   **Date:** _______________

Say the name of each picture. Color four things that start with **E**.

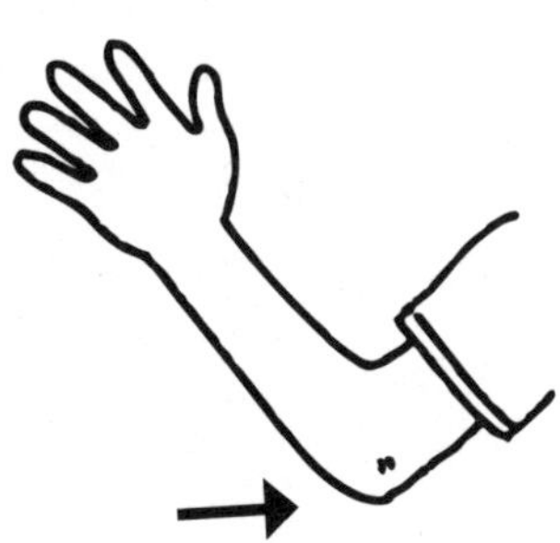

Cut along the dashed lines. Weave the strip through the slots, as shown. Slide the strip to see the pictures and words.

fan

fish

five

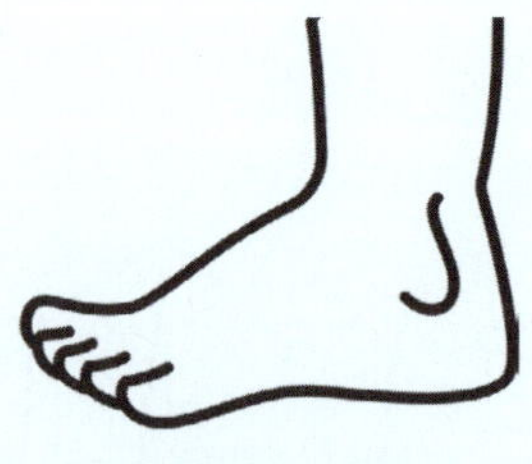

foot

Name: ___________________________   **Date:** ___________________

Trace **Ff**. Say the /f/ sound.

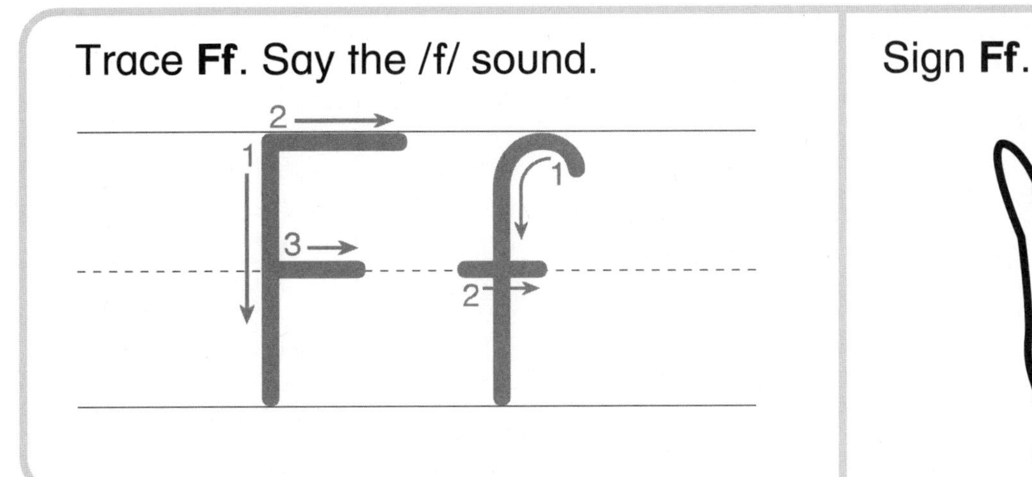

Sign **Ff**.

Say the name of each picture. What sound do you hear at the beginning?
Write **Ff** next to each picture.

Trace the **F** and **f**'s.

Five fast fish flee.

Name: ______________________________   **Date:** ______________

Say the name of each picture. Color four things that start with **F**.

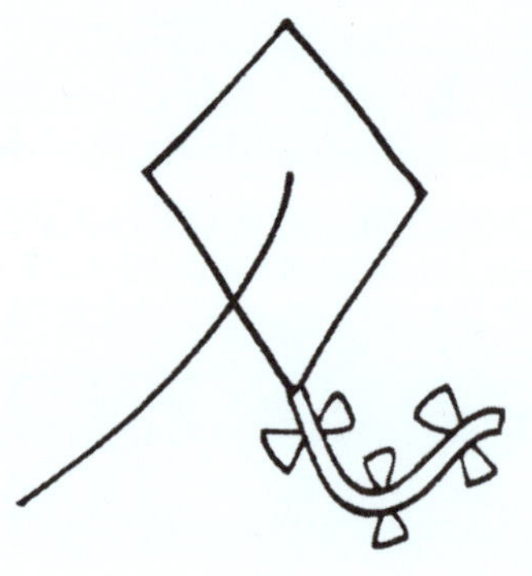

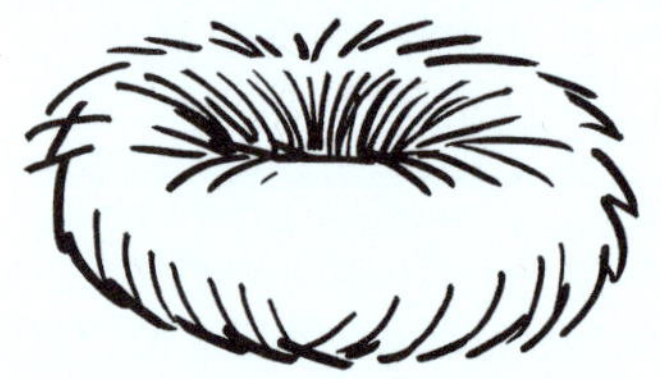

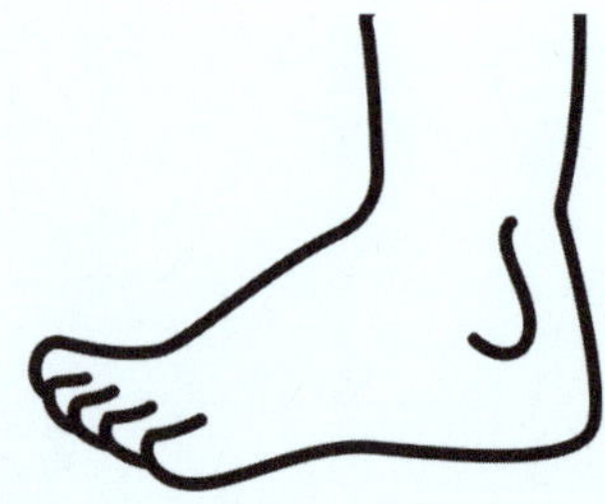

Cut along the dashed lines. Weave the strip through the slots, as shown. Slide the strip to see the pictures and words.

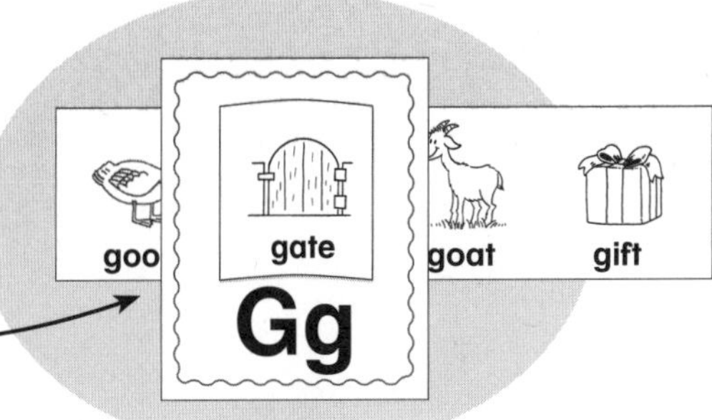

goose

gate

goat

gift

Name: _______________________________   **Date:** ___________________

Trace **Gg**. Say the /g/ sound.

Sign **Gg**.

Say the name of each picture. What sound do you hear at the beginning? Write **Gg** next to each picture.

Trace the **G** and **g**'s.

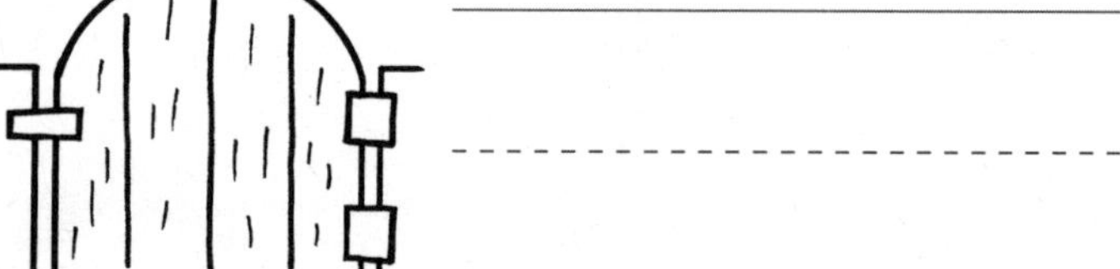

Name: ___________________________________   **Date:** ___________________

Say the name of each picture. Color four things that start with **G**.

Cut along the dashed lines. Weave the strip through the slots, as shown. Slide the strip to see the pictures and words.

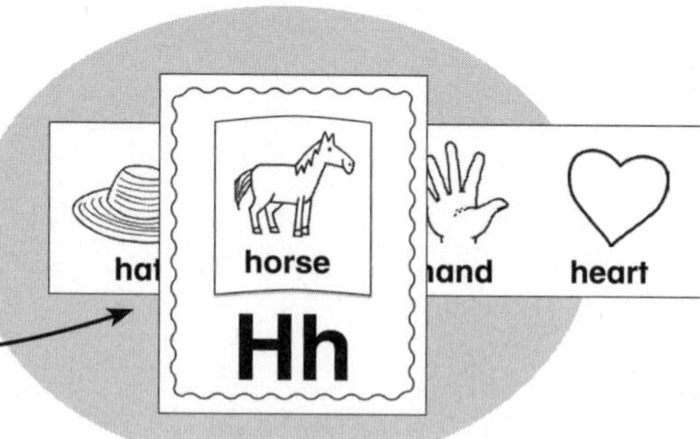

hat

horse

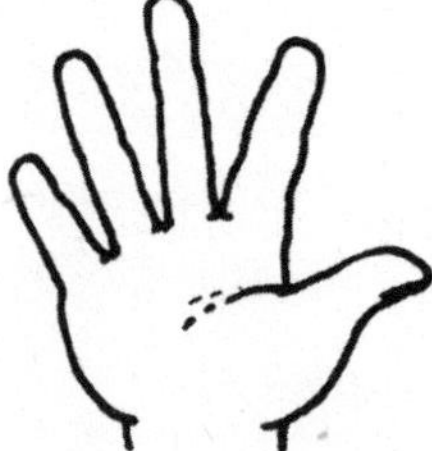

hand

heart

Name: ___________________________   **Date:** ___________

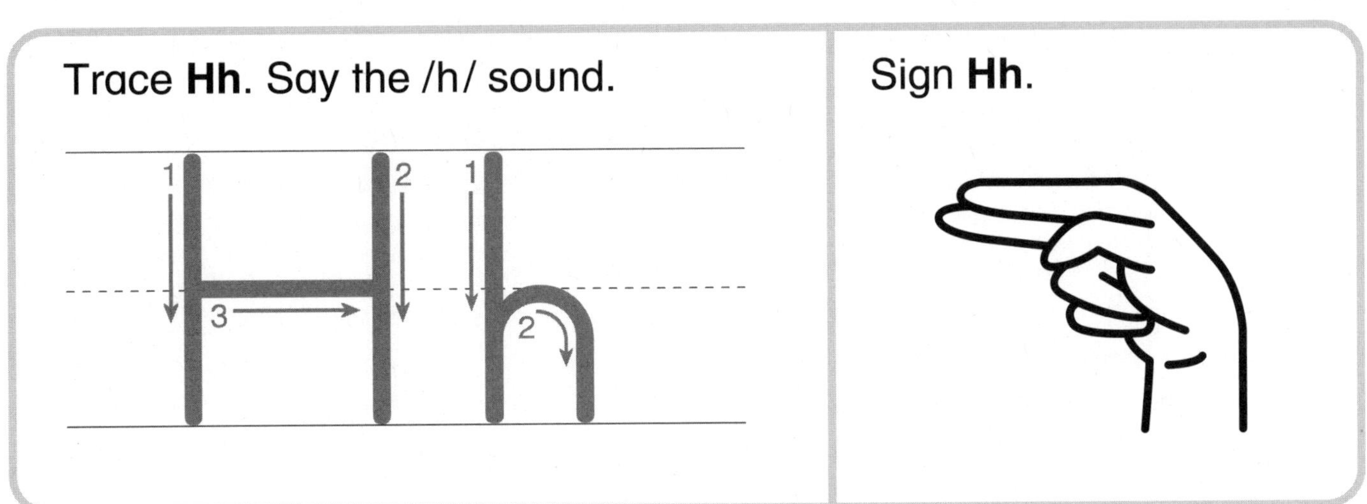

Say the name of each picture. What sound do you hear at the beginning?
Write **Hh** next to each picture.

Trace the **H** and **h**'s.

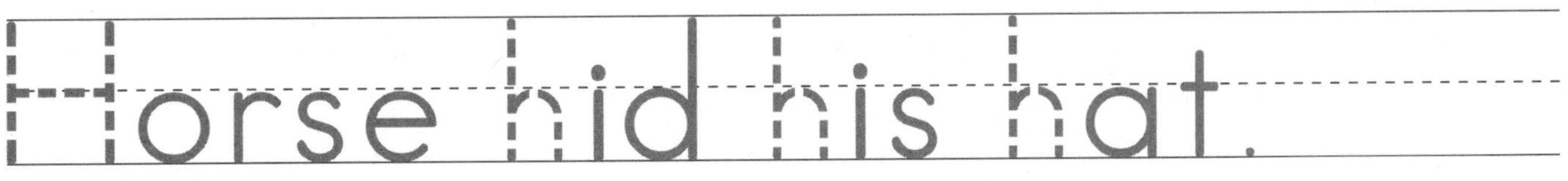

Name: _______________________ **Date:** _______________

Say the name of each picture. Color four things that start with **H**.

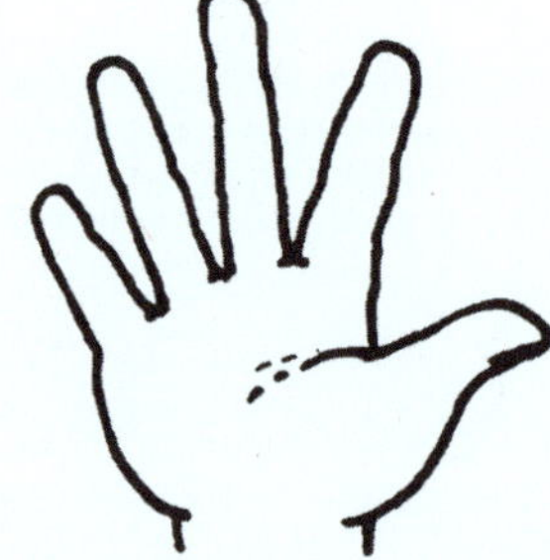  

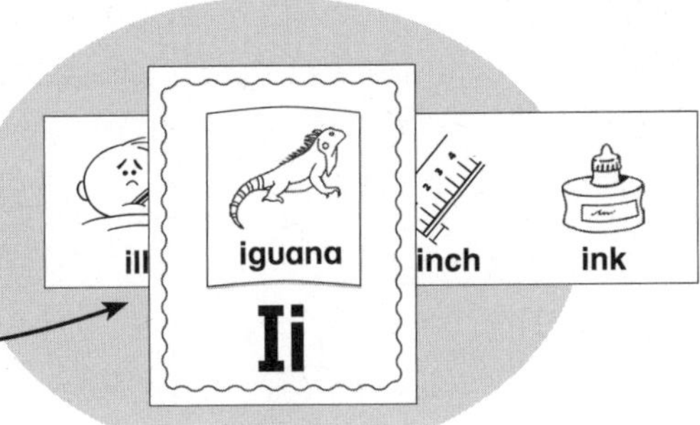

Cut along the dashed lines. Weave the strip through the slots, as shown. Slide the strip to see the pictures and words.

ill

iguana

inch

ink

Name: _______________________________   **Date:** _______________

Trace **Ii**. Say the /i/ sound.

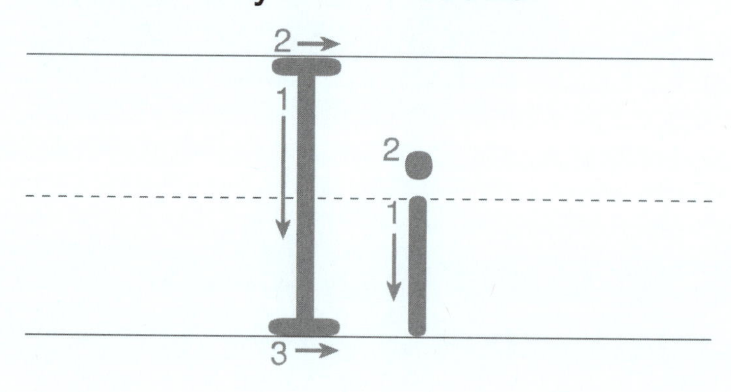

Sign **Ii**.

Say the name of each picture. What sound do you hear at the beginning?
Write **Ii** next to each picture.

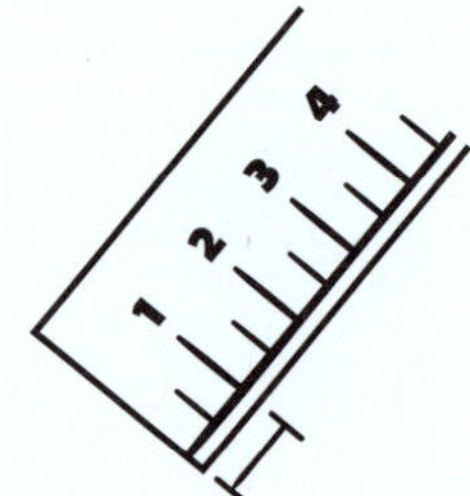

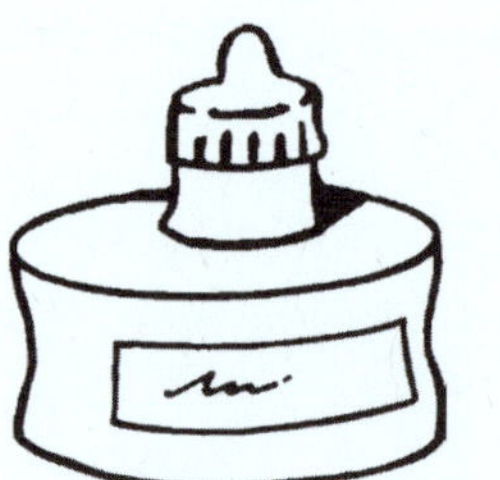

Trace the **I**'s and **i**'s.

Izzy Iguana is ill.

Name: ___________________________ **Date:** _______________

Say the name of each picture. Color four things that start with **I**.

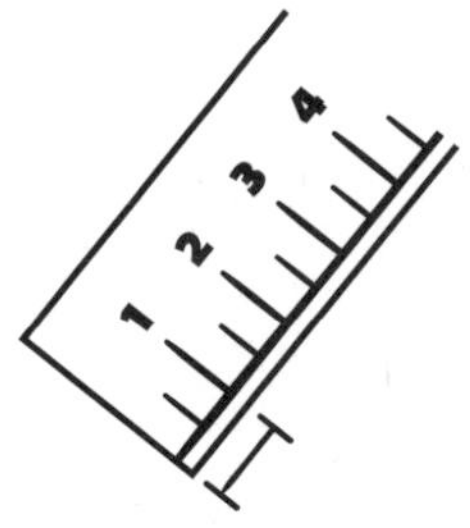  

Cut along the dashed lines. Weave the strip through the slots, as shown. Slide the strip to see the pictures and words.

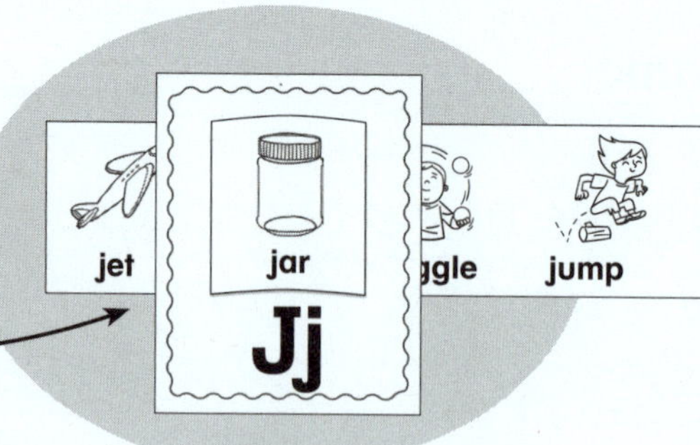

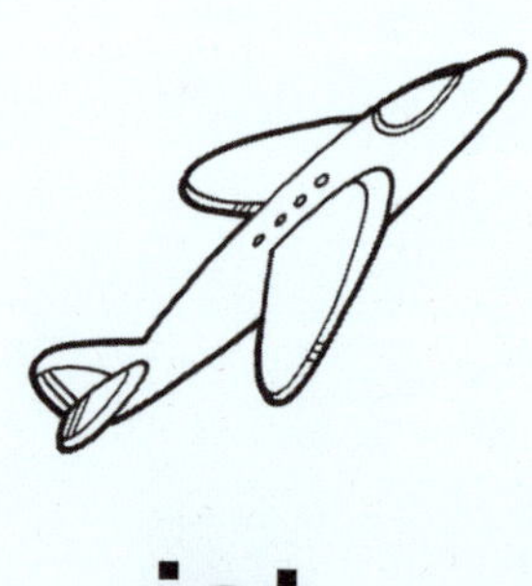

jet

jar

juggle

jump

Name: _______________________ **Date:** _______________

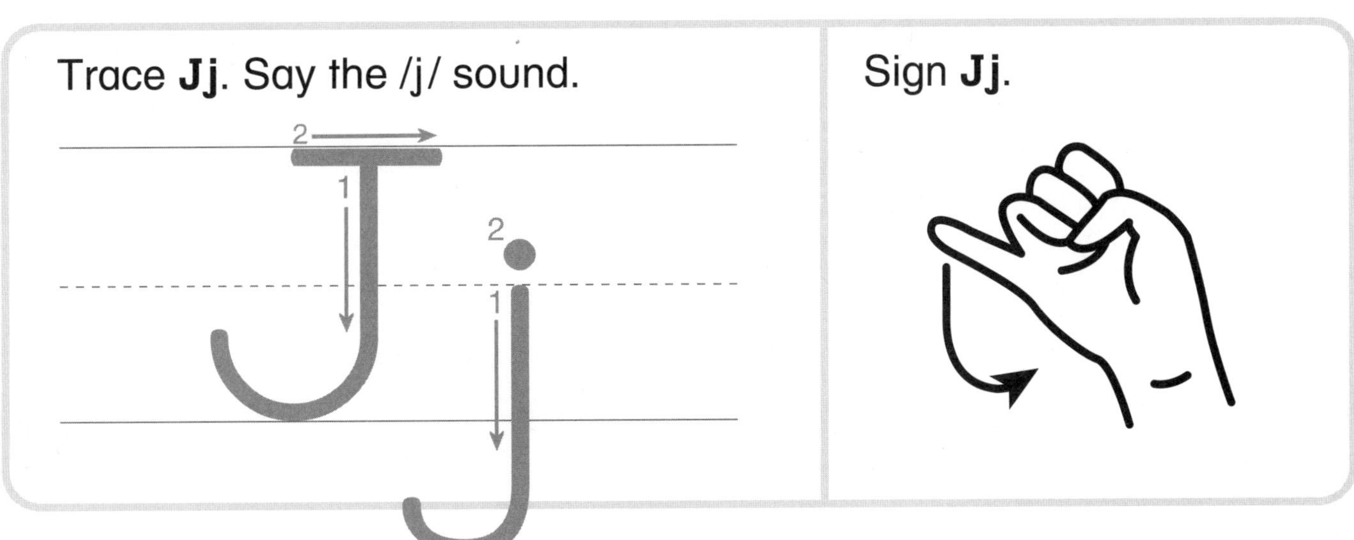

Say the name of each picture. What sound do you hear at the beginning? Write **Jj** next to each picture.

Trace the **J** and **j**'s.

Name: _________________________________ **Date:** _______________

Say the name of each picture. Color four things that start with **J**.

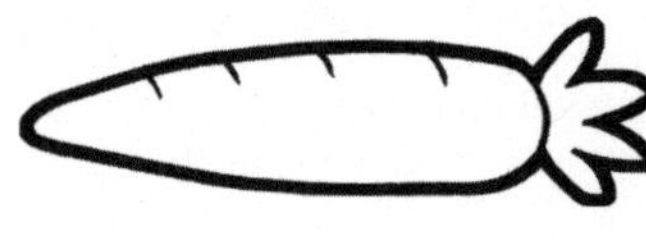

Cut along the dashed lines. Weave the strip through the slots, as shown. Slide the strip to see the pictures and words.

key

koala

kite

kick

Name: __________________________________   **Date:** ________________

Trace **Kk**. Say the /k/ sound.

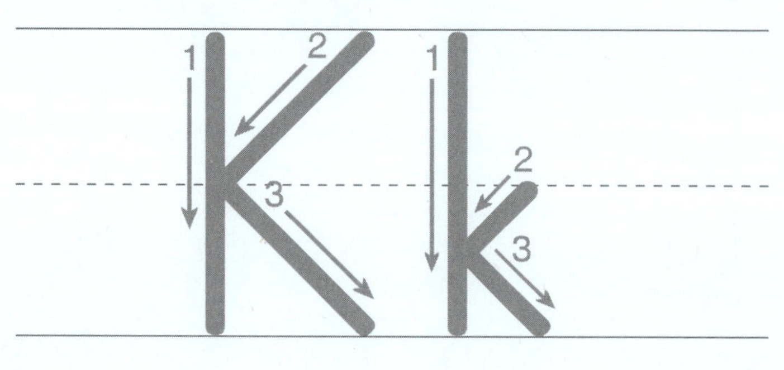

Sign **Kk**.

Say the name of each picture. What sound do you hear at the beginning?
Write **Kk** next to each picture.

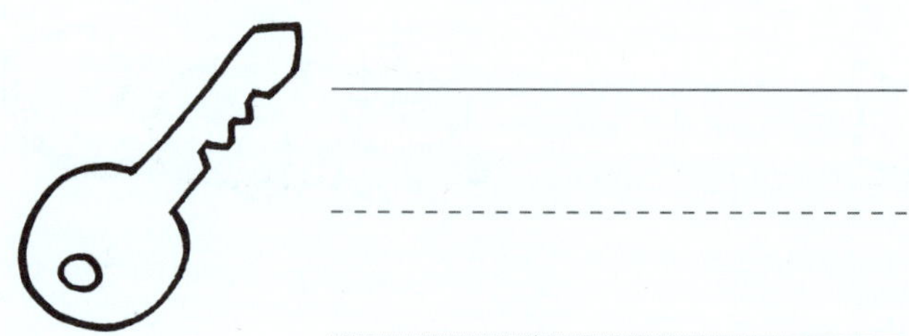

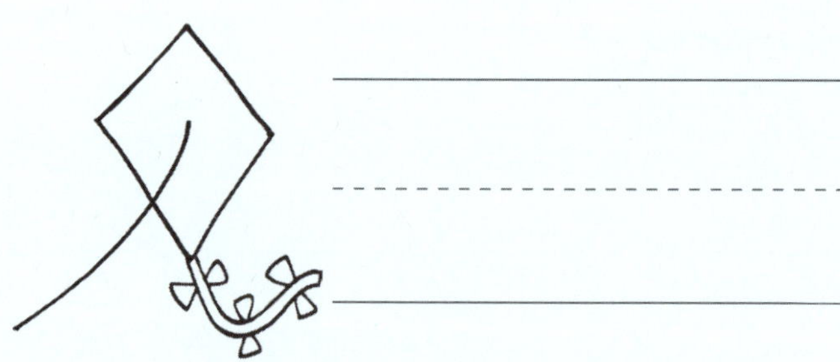

Trace the **K** and **k**'s.

Kids like pink kites.

Name: _________________________   **Date:** _________________________

Say the name of each picture. Color four things that start with **K**.

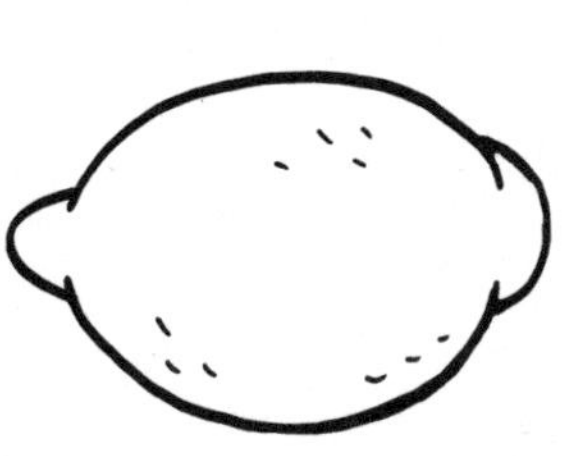
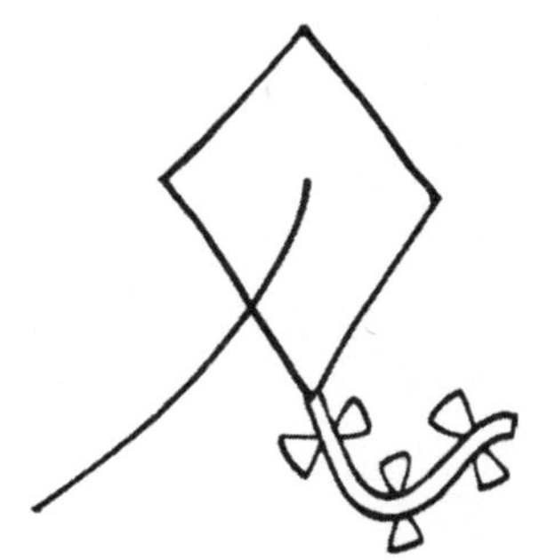

Cut along the dashed lines. Weave the strip through the slots, as shown. Slide the strip to see the pictures and words.

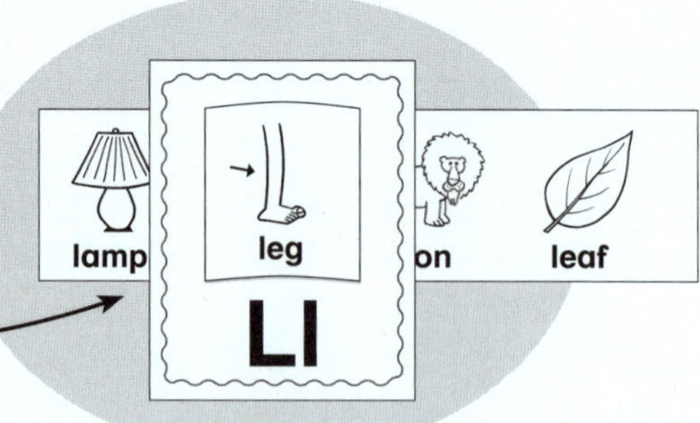

lamp

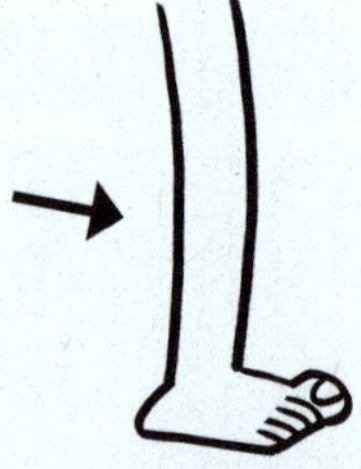

leg

lion

leaf

Name: _________________________ **Date:** _______________

Trace **Ll**. Say the /l/ sound.

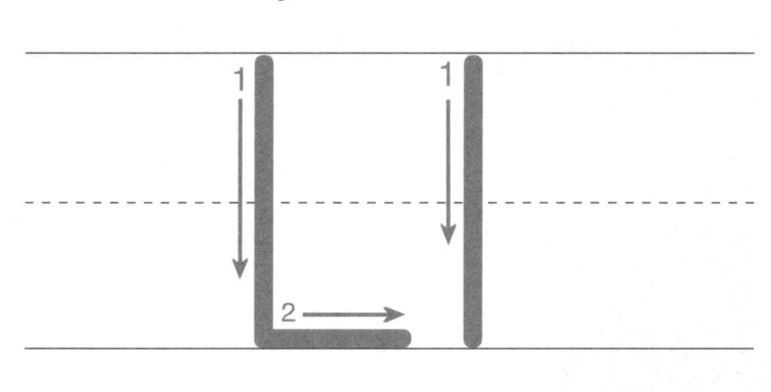

Sign **Ll**.

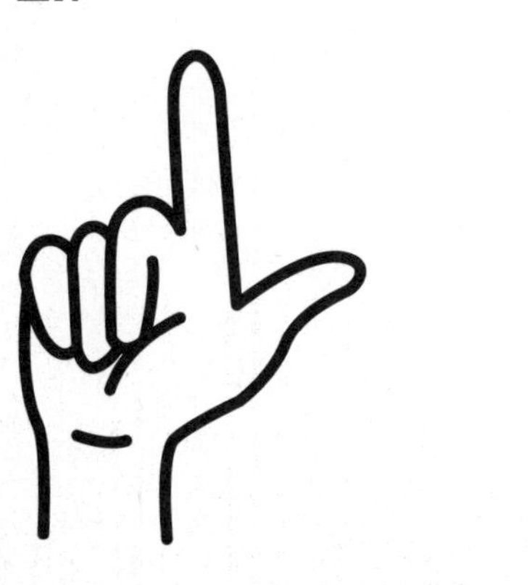

Say the name of each picture. What sound do you hear at the beginning? Write **Ll** next to each picture.

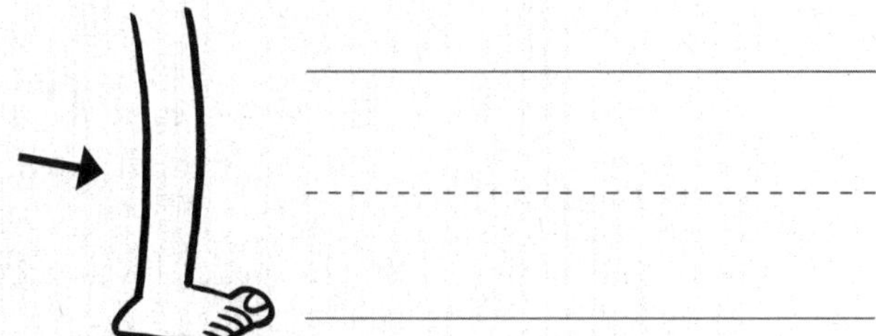

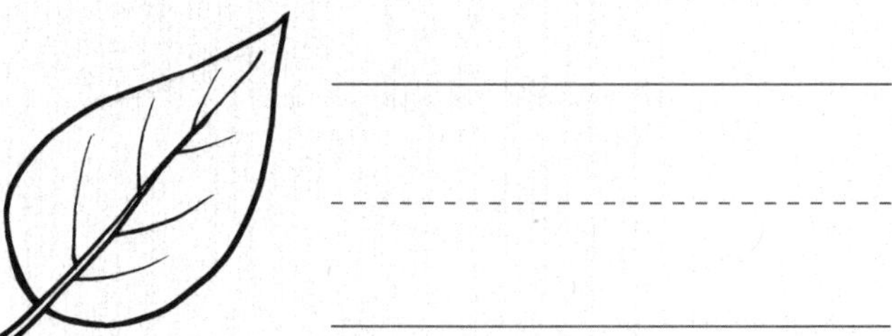

Trace the **L** and **l**'s.

Lion lit a large lamp.

Name: ____ **Date:** _______________

Say the name of each picture. Color four things that start with **L**.

  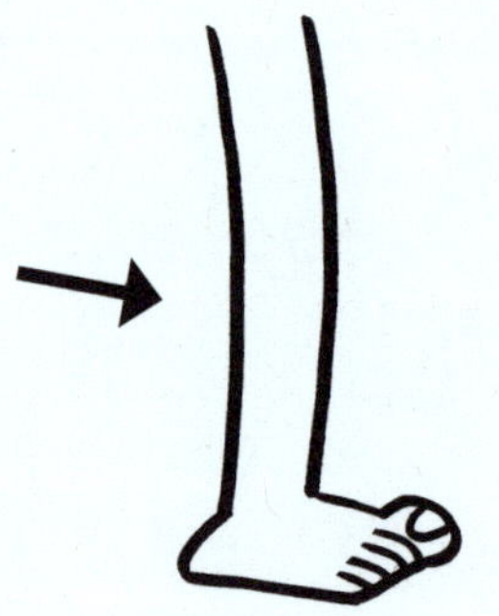

 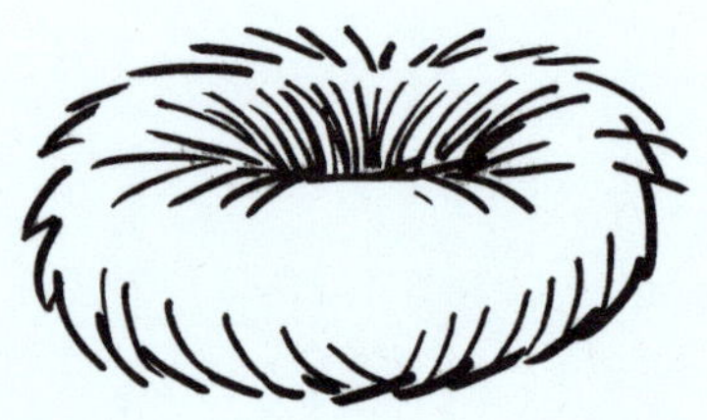

Cut along the dashed lines. Weave the strip through the slots, as shown. Slide the strip to see the pictures and words.

moon

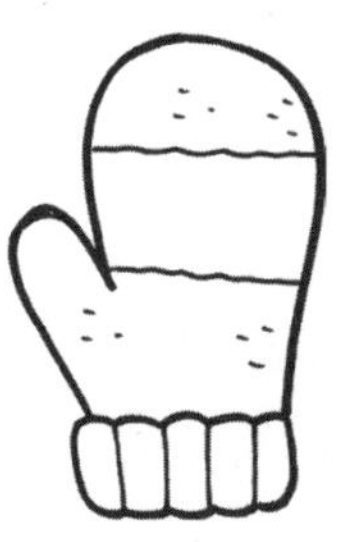

mitten

monkey

map

Name: ________________________________   **Date:** ____________

Trace **Mm**. Say the /m/ sound.

Sign **Mm**.

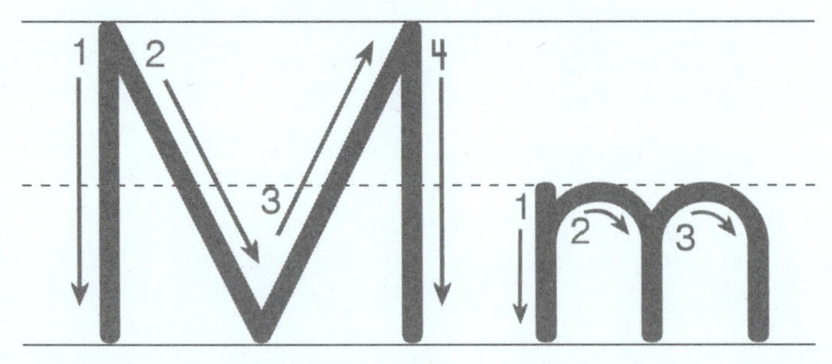

Say the name of each picture. What sound do you hear at the beginning? Write **Mm** next to each picture.

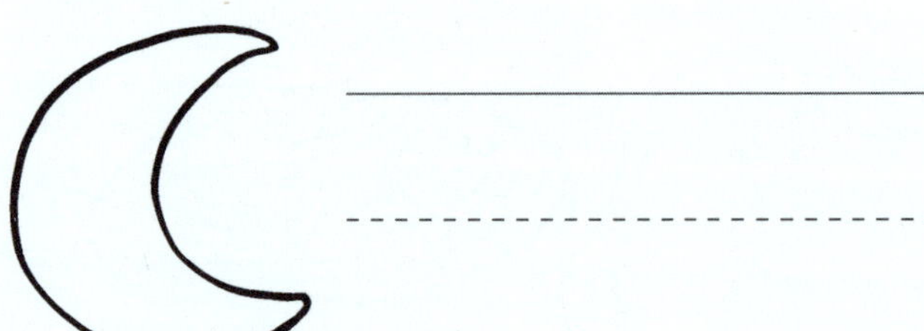

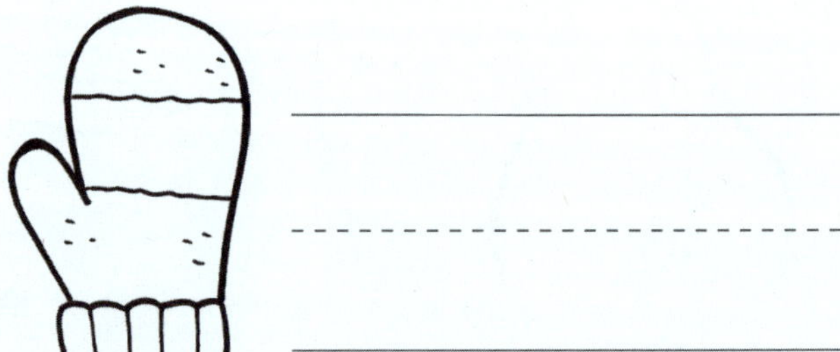

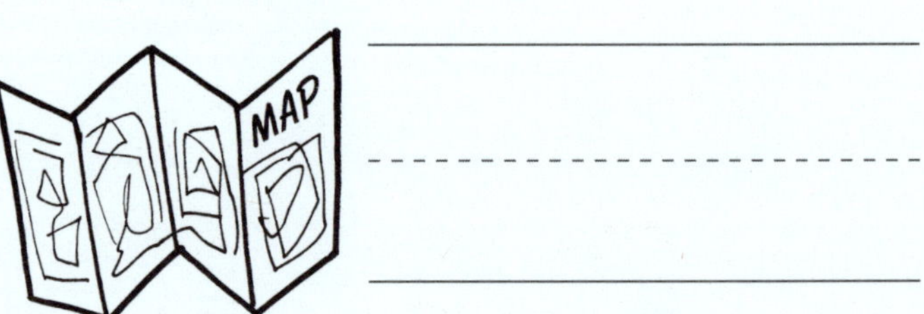

Trace the **M** and **m**'s.

Monkey made a map.

Name: ___________________________   **Date:** _______________

Say the name of each picture. Color four things that start with **M**.

Cut along the dashed lines. Weave the strip through the slots, as shown. Slide the strip to see the pictures and words.

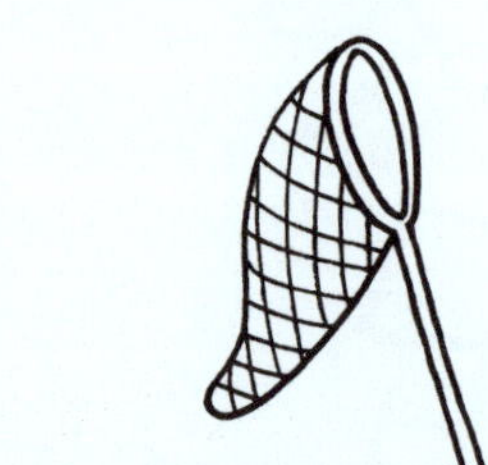

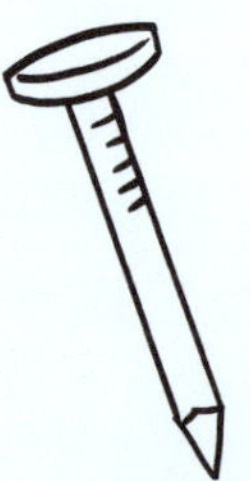

net　　**nine**　　**nail**　　**nest**

Name: _______________________________   **Date:** _______________

Trace **Nn**. Say the /n/ sound.

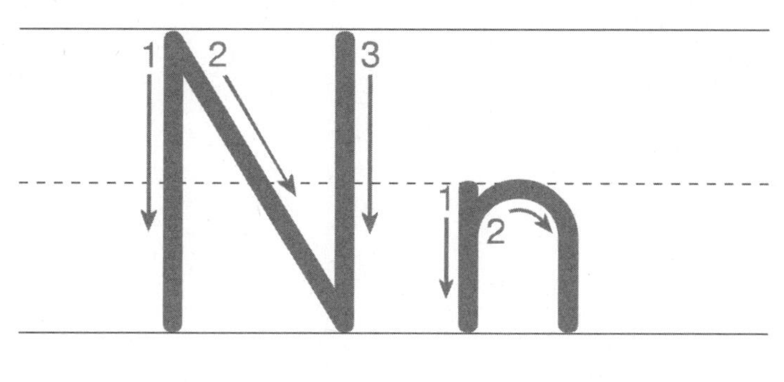

Sign **Nn**.

Say the name of each picture. What sound do you hear at the beginning? Write **Nn** next to each picture.

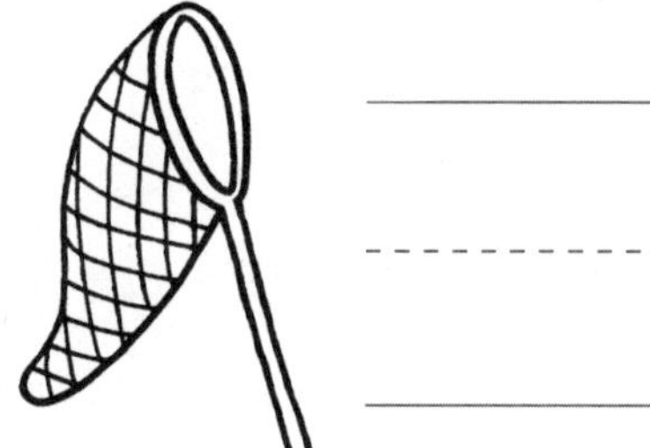

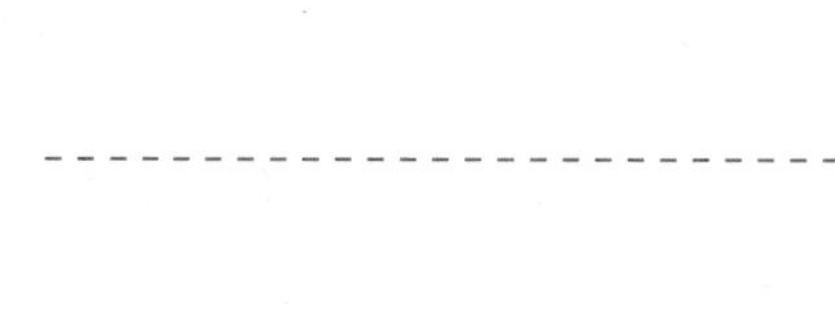

Trace the **N** and **n**'s.

Ned needs nine nets.

Name: ______________________________   **Date:** ______________

Say the name of each picture. Color four things that start with **N**.

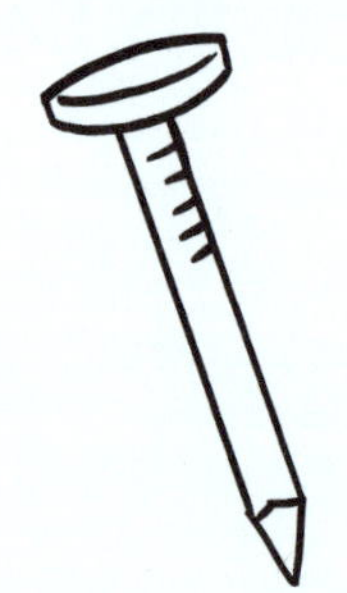
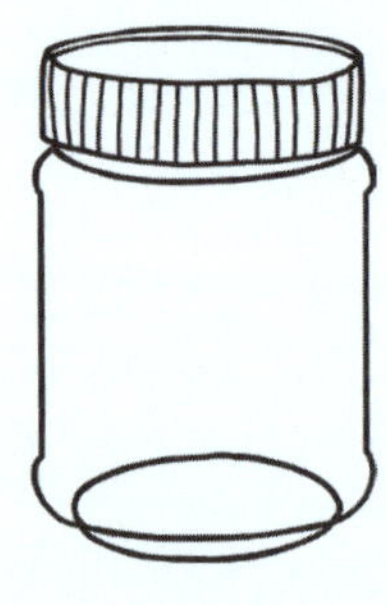

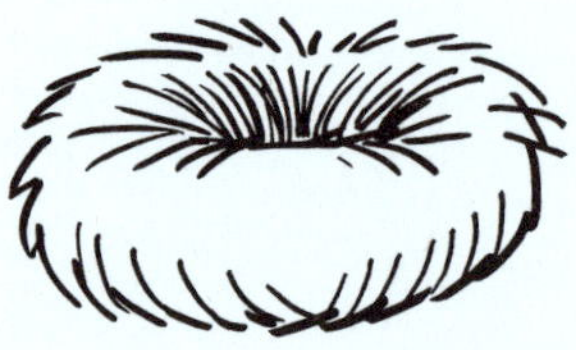
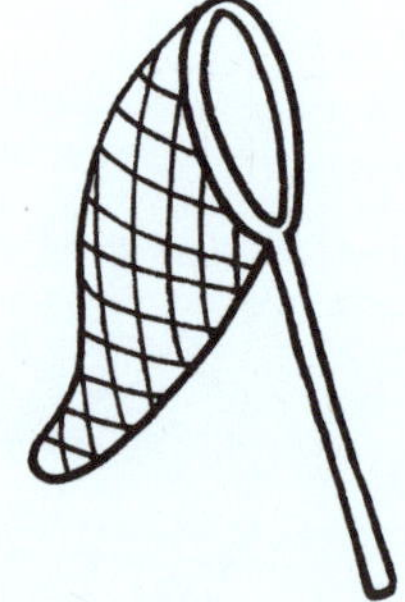

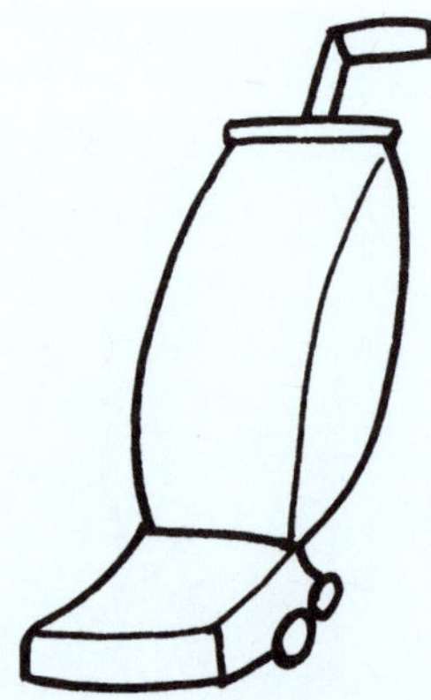

Cut along the dashed lines. Weave the strip through the slots, as shown. Slide the strip to see the pictures and words.

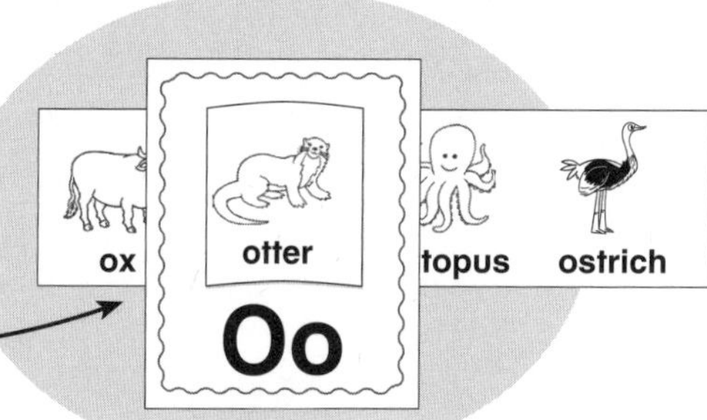

ox

otter

octopus

ostrich

Name: _______________________________   **Date:** _______________

Trace **Oo**. Say the /o/ sound.

Sign **Oo**.

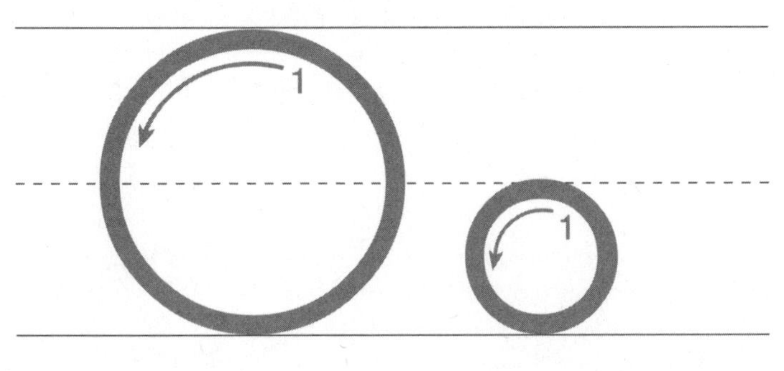

Say the name of each picture. What sound do you hear at the beginning? Write **Oo** next to each picture.

Trace the **O**'s and **o**'s.

Ox and Otter jog.

Name: _______________________________ **Date:** _______________

Say the name of each picture. Color four things that start with **O**.

Cut along the dashed lines. Weave the strip through the slots, as shown. Slide the strip to see the pictures and words.

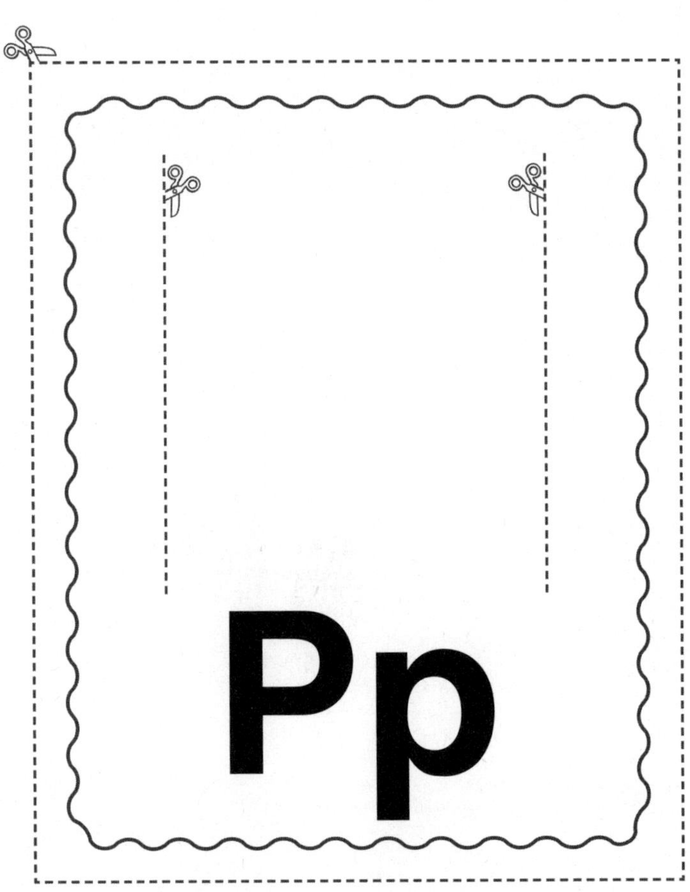

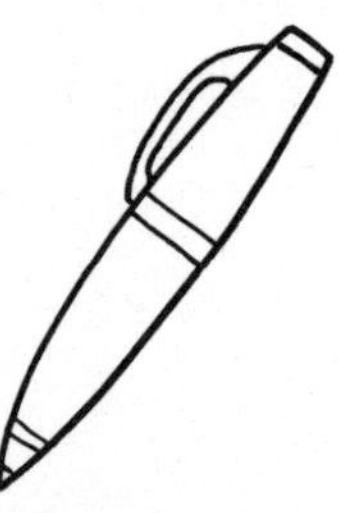

pen

panda

pumpkin

pizza

Name: _________________________________   **Date:** _______________

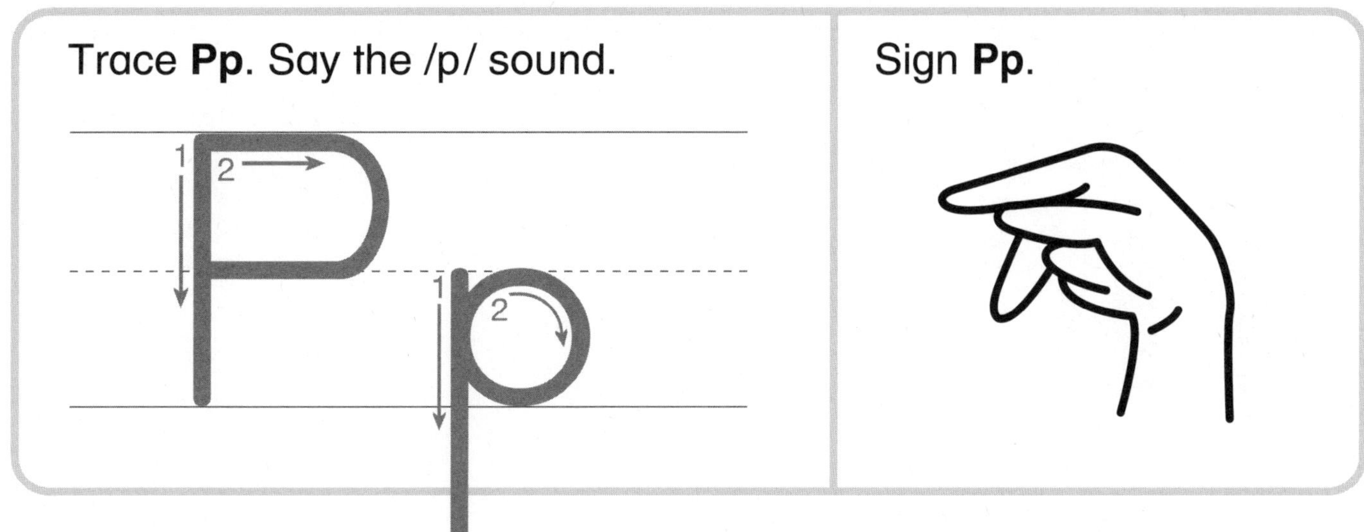

Trace **Pp**. Say the /p/ sound.

Sign **Pp**.

Say the name of each picture. What sound do you hear at the beginning?
Write **Pp** next to each picture.

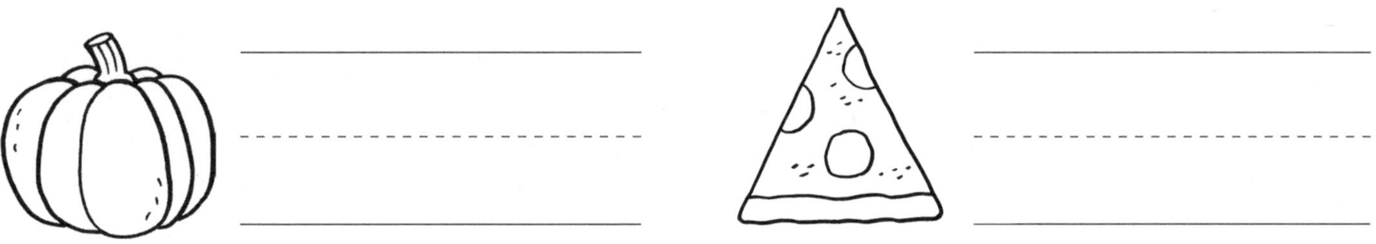

Trace the **P** and **p**'s.

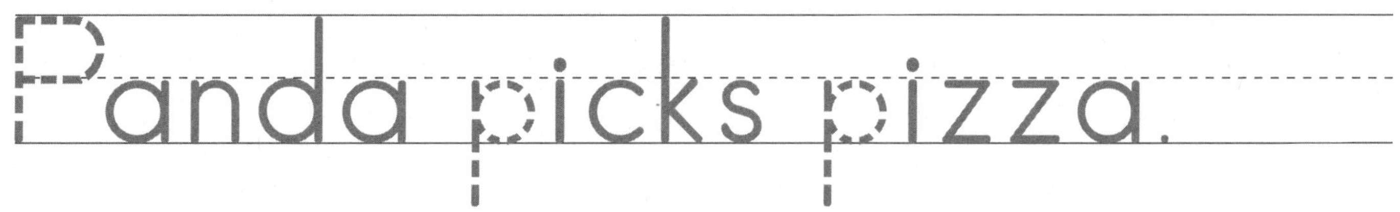

Name: _______________________________   **Date:** _______________

Say the name of each picture. Color four things that start with **P**.

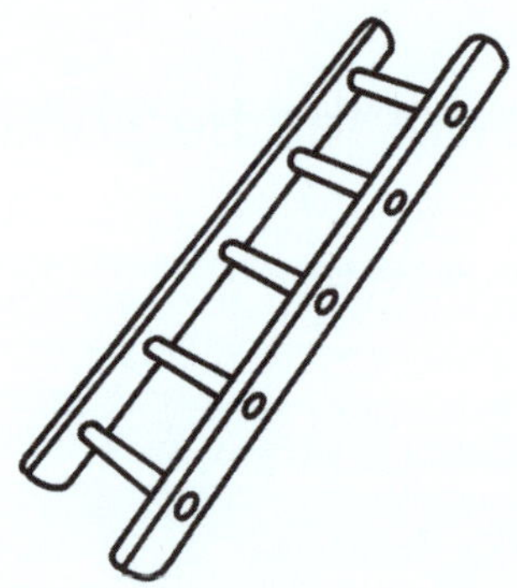

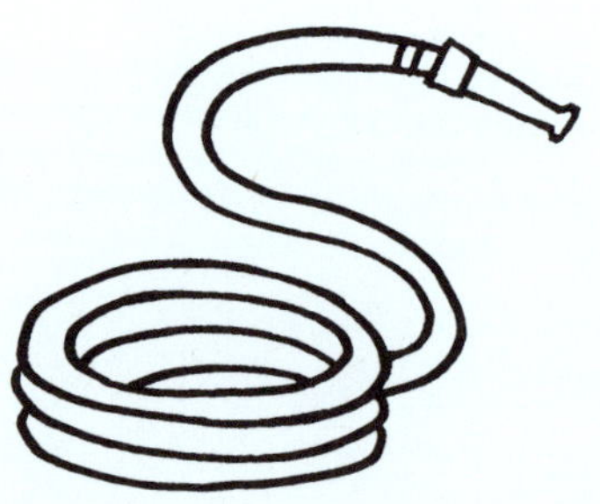

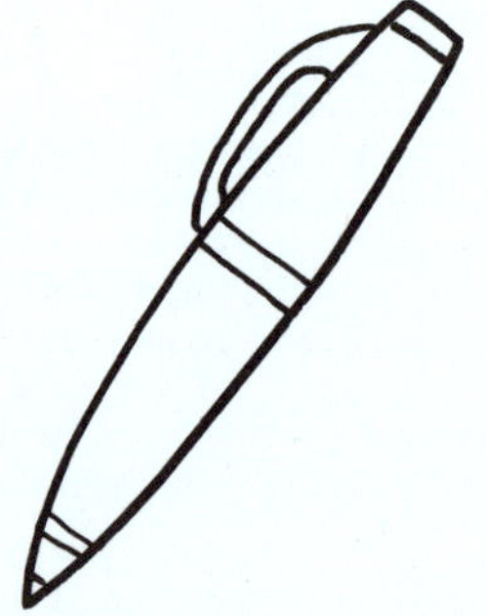

Cut along the dashed lines. Weave the strip through the slots, as shown. Slide the strip to see the pictures and words.

queen

quarter

quiet

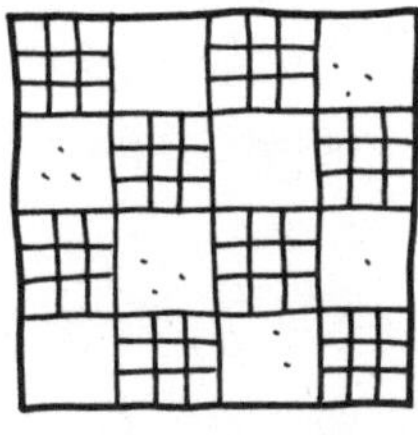

quilt

Name: ________________________________   **Date:** ________________

Trace **Qq**. Say the /k/ sound.

Sign **Qq**.

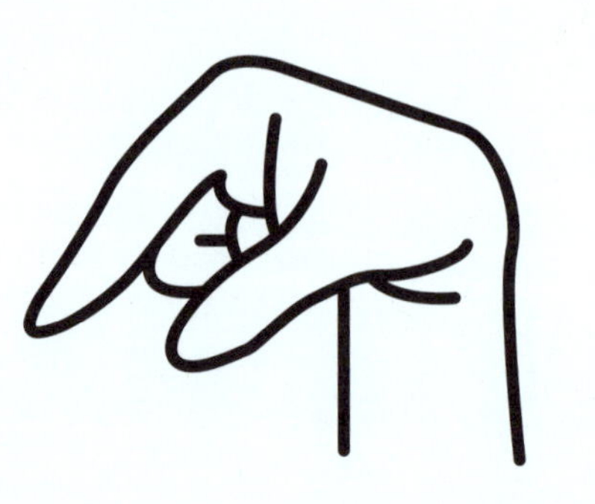

Say the name of each picture. What sound do you hear at the beginning? Write **Qq** next to each picture.

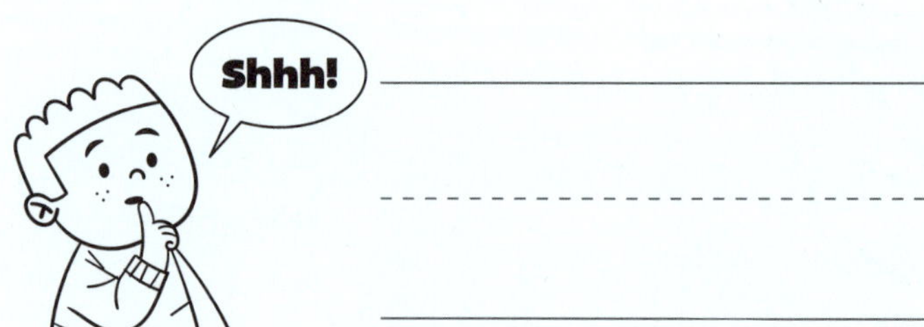

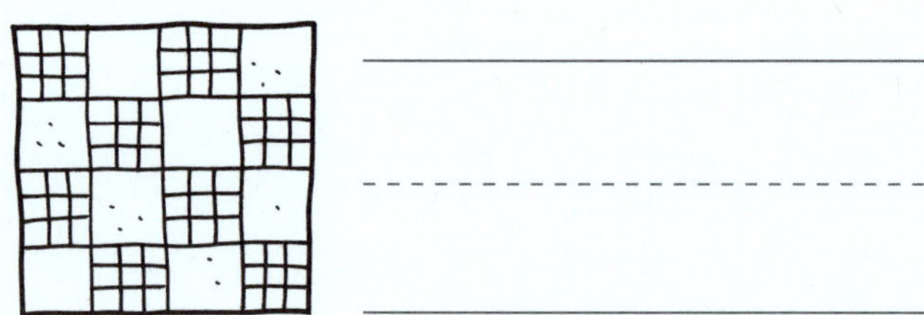

Trace the **Q** and **q**'s.

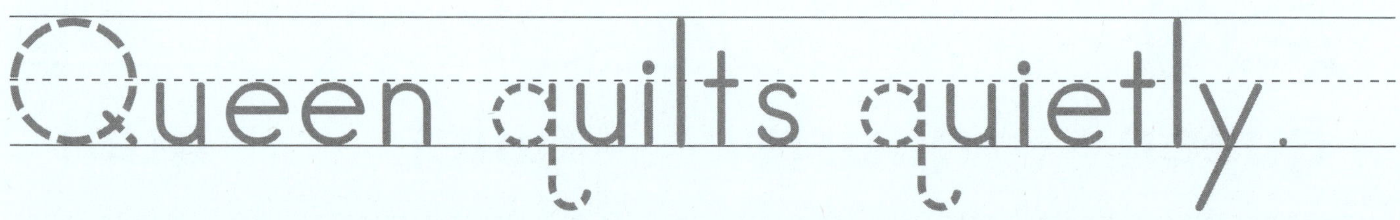

Name: _______________________   **Date:** _______________

Say the name of each picture. Color four things that start with **Q**.

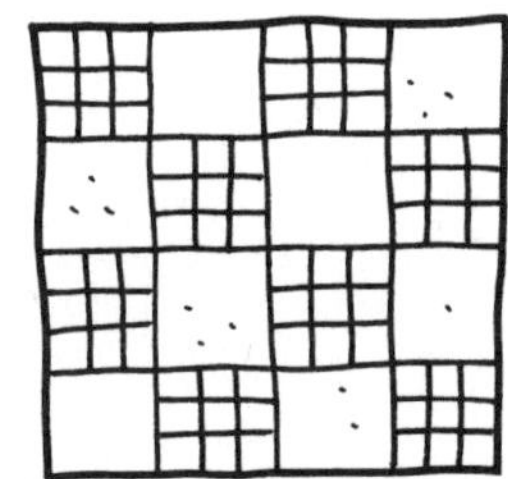

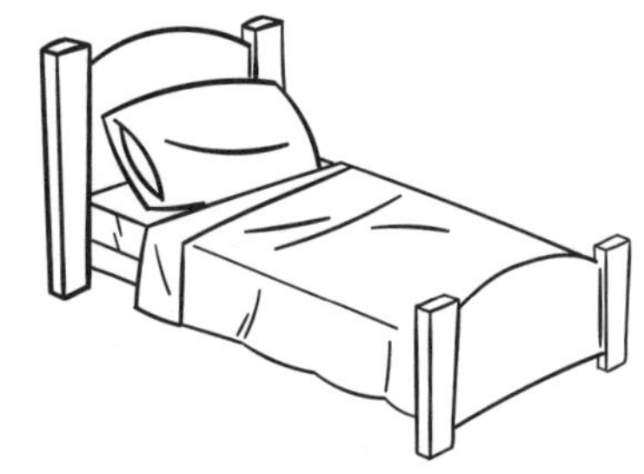

Cut along the dashed lines. Weave the strip through the slots, as shown. Slide the strip to see the pictures and words.

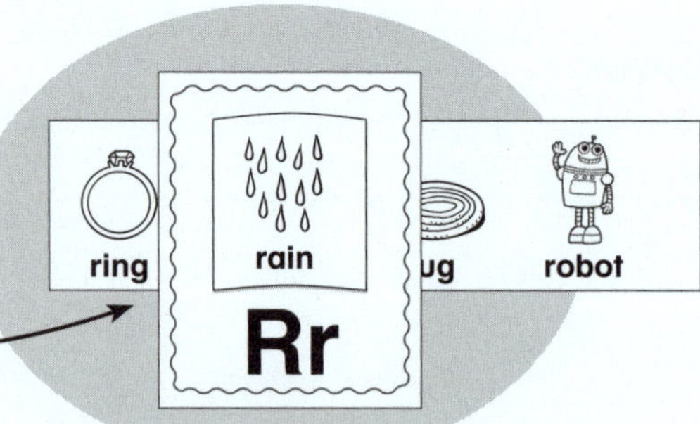

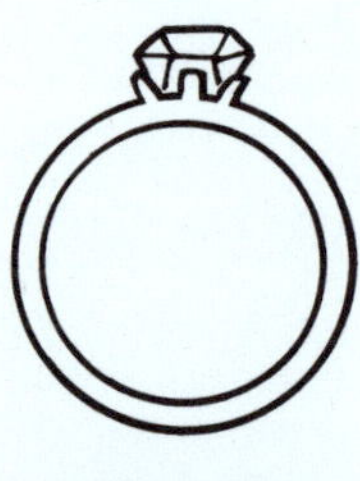

ring

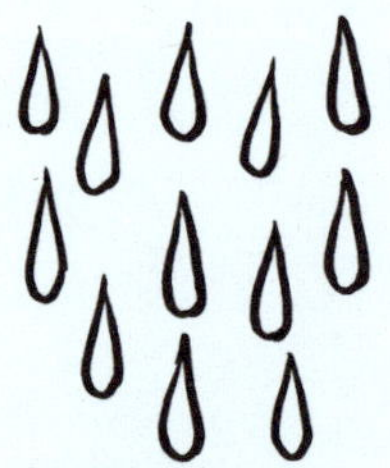

rain

rug

robot

Name: ___________________________   **Date:** _______________

Trace **Rr**. Say the /r/ sound.

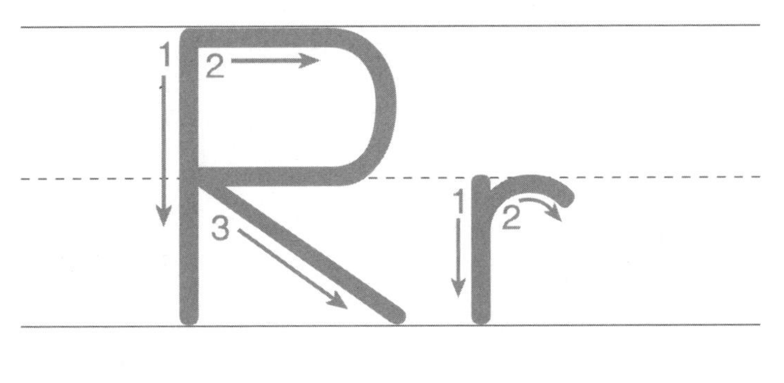

Sign **Rr**.

Say the name of each picture. What sound do you hear at the beginning? Write **Rr** next to each picture.

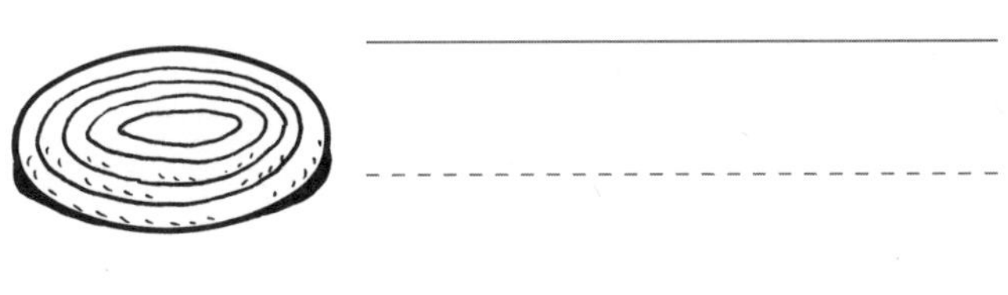

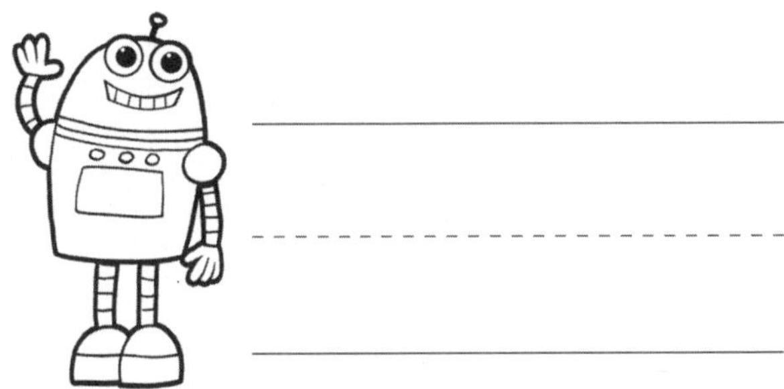

Trace the **R** and **r**'s.

Robot ran in the rain.

Say the name of each picture. Color four things that start with **R**.

Cut along the dashed lines. Weave the strip through the slots, as shown. Slide the strip to see the pictures and words.

saw

seal

sun

six

Name: _______________________________   **Date:** _______________

Trace **Ss**. Say the /s/ sound.

Sign **Ss**.

Say the name of each picture. What sound do you hear at the beginning?
Write **Ss** next to each picture.

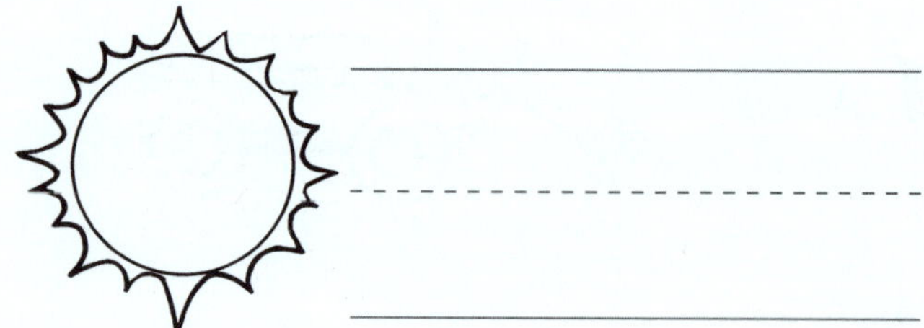

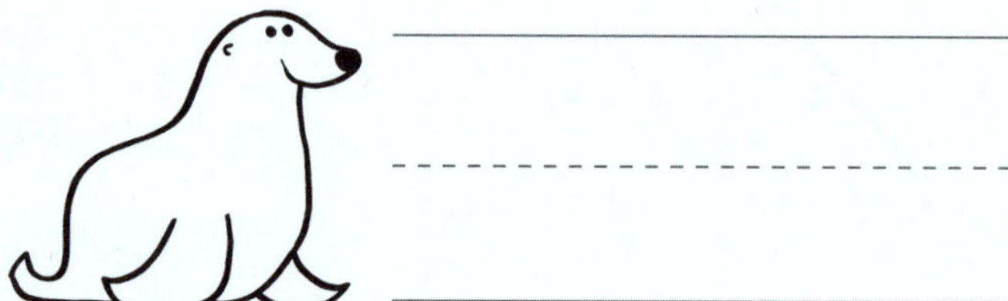

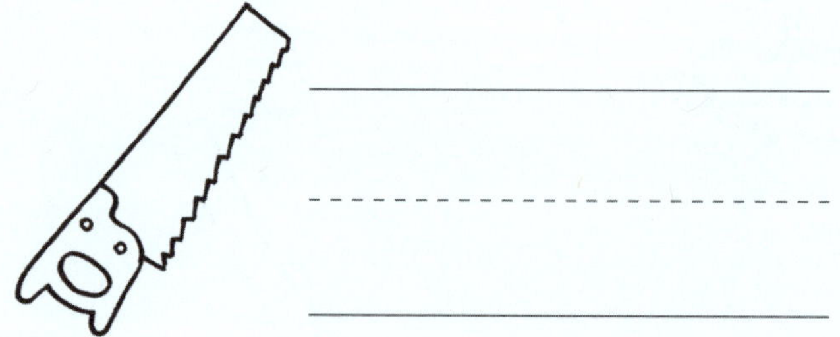

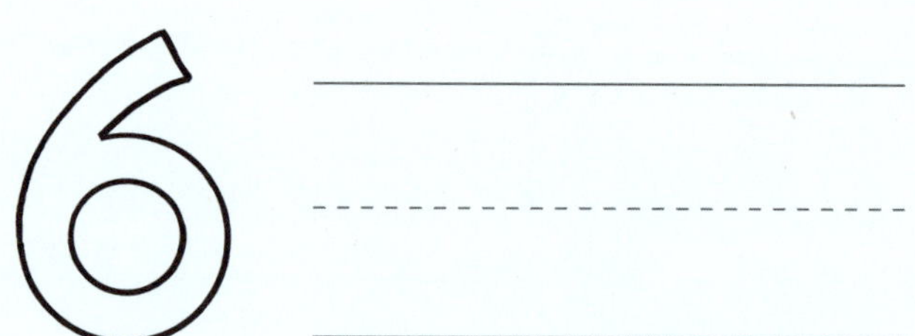

Trace the **S** and **s**'s.

Sal saw six seals.

Name: _______________________ **Date:** _______________

Say the name of each picture. Color four things that start with **S**.

Cut along the dashed lines. Weave the strip through the slots, as shown. Slide the strip to see the pictures and words.

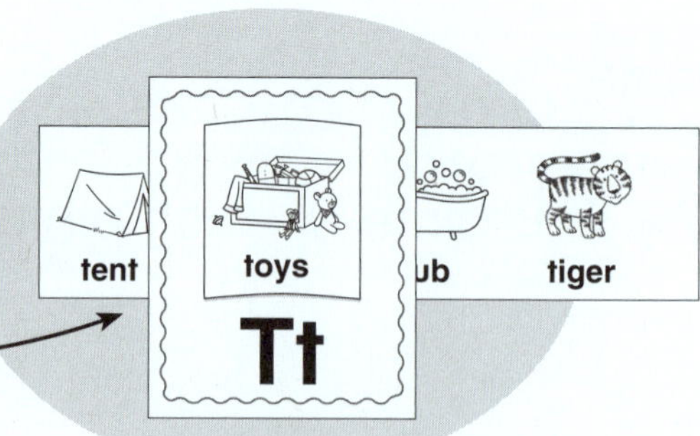

Tt

tent

toys

tub

tiger

Name: _______________________   **Date:** _______________

Trace **Tt**. Say the /t/ sound.

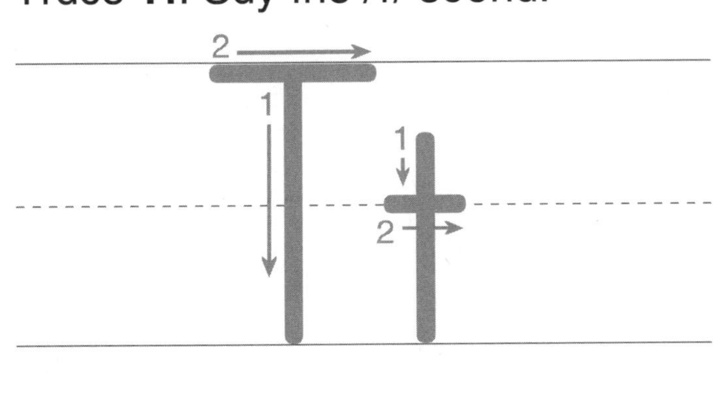

Sign **Tt**.

Say the name of each picture. What sound do you hear at the beginning?
Write **Tt** next to each picture.

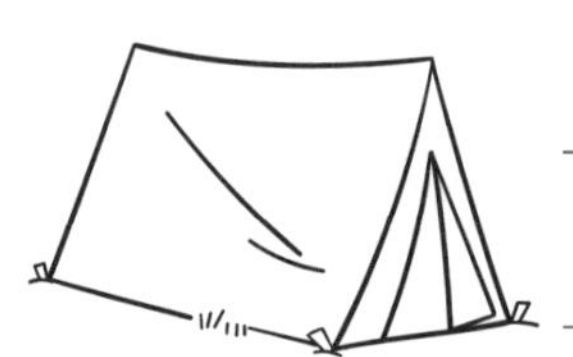

Trace the **T** and **t**'s.

Tiger took the toys.

Name: _________________________________   **Date:** _____________

Say the name of each picture. Color four things that start with **T**.

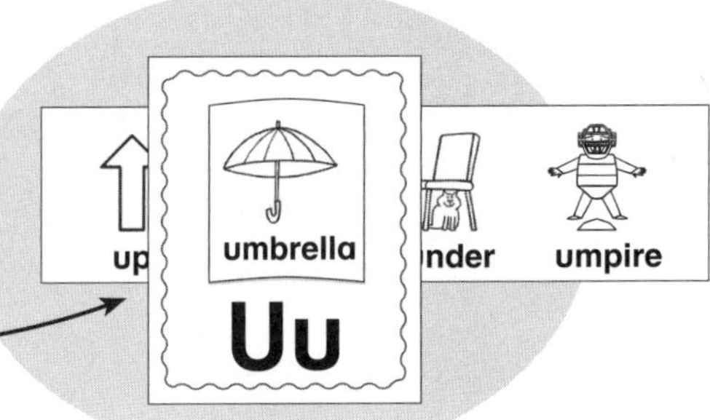

Cut along the dashed lines. Weave the strip through the slots, as shown. Slide the strip to see the pictures and words.

up

umbrella

under

umpire

Name: ___________________________________   **Date:** _______________

Trace **Uu**. Say the /u/ sound.

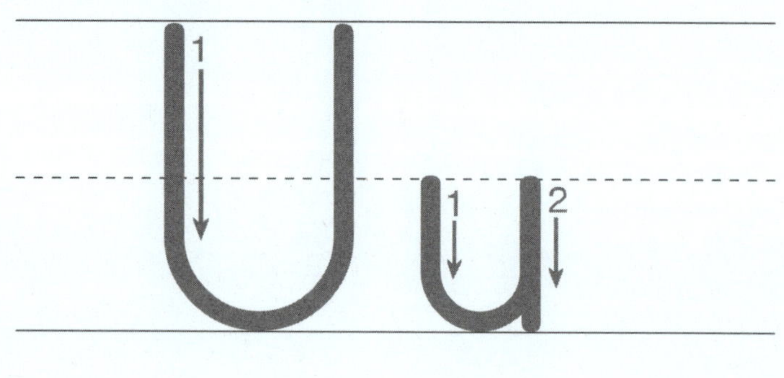

Sign **Uu**.

Say the name of each picture. What sound do you hear at the beginning? Write **Uu** next to each picture.

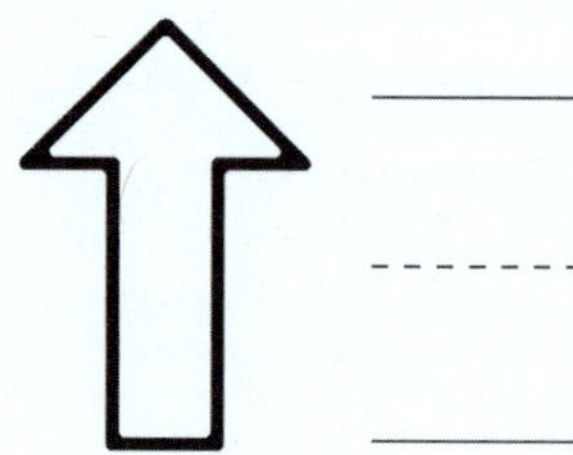

Trace the **U** and **u**'s.

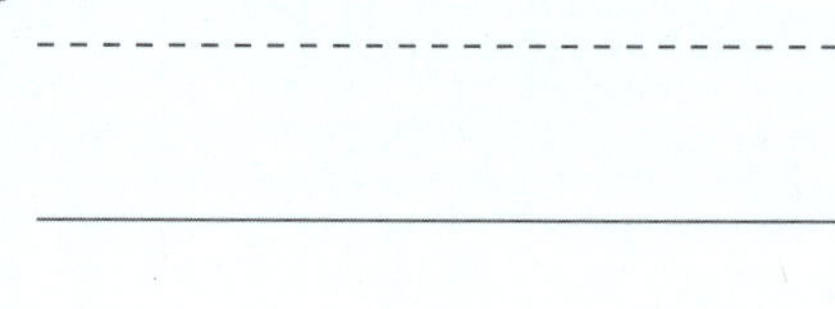

Up went the umbrella.

Name: _______________________ **Date:** _______________________

Say the name of each picture. Color four things that start with **U**.

Cut along the dashed lines. Weave the strip through the slots, as shown. Slide the strip to see the pictures and words.

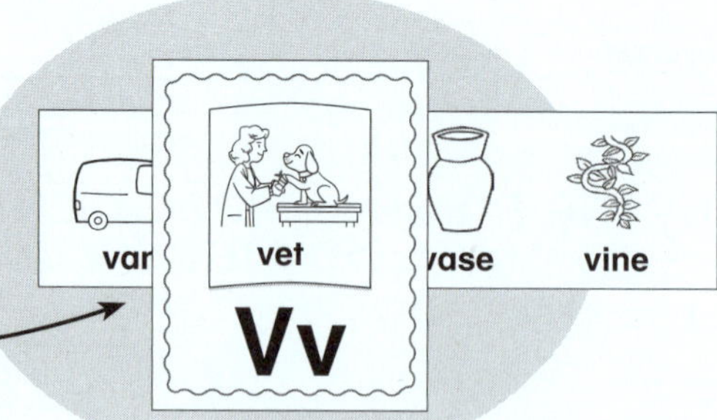

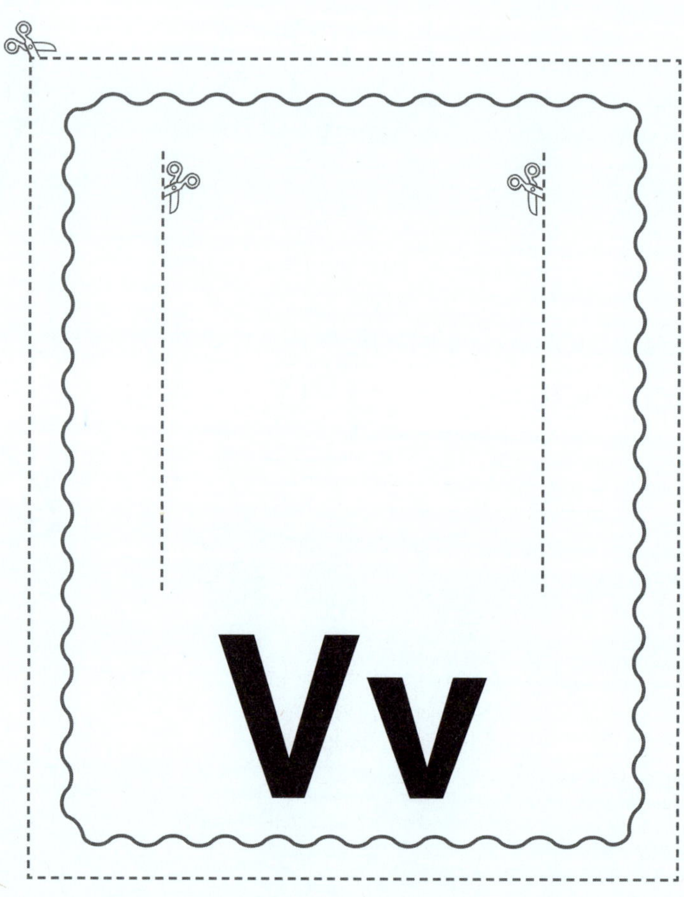

van

vet

vase

vine

Name: ________________________________   **Date:** ________________

Trace **Vv**. Say the /v/ sound.

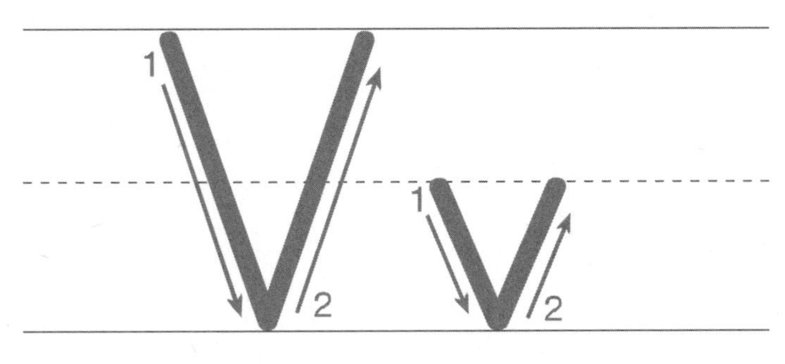

Sign **Vv**.

Say the name of each picture. What sound do you hear at the beginning?
Write **Vv** next to each picture.

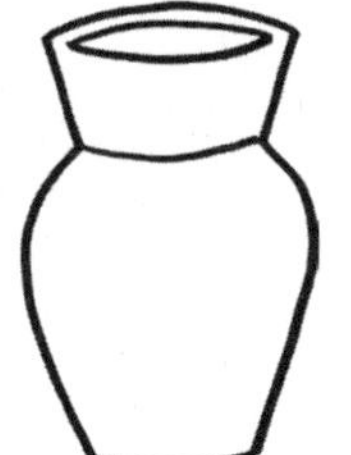

Trace the **V** and **v**'s.

Viv visited a vet.

Name: ___________________________________   **Date:** ___________________

Say the name of each picture. Color four things that start with **V**.

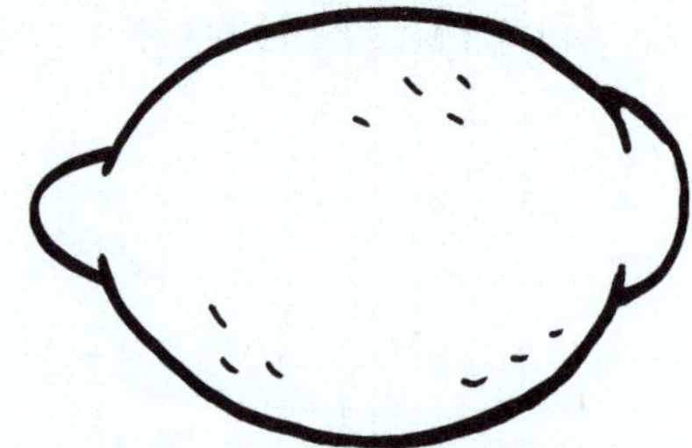

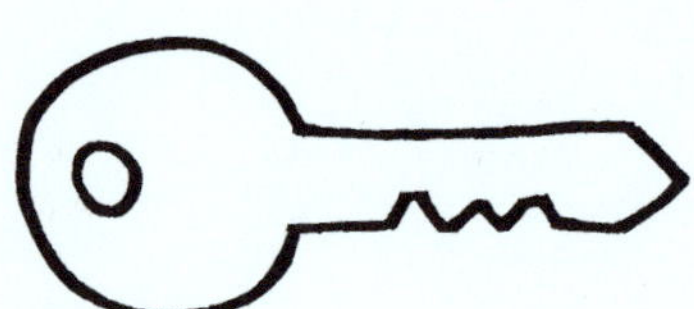

Cut along the dashed lines. Weave the strip through the slots, as shown. Slide the strip to see the pictures and words.

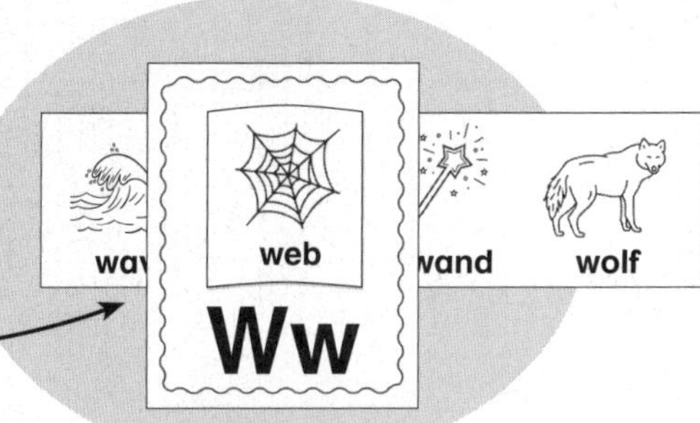

wave

web

wand

wolf

Name: ____________________________   **Date:** ____________________

Trace **Ww**. Say the /w/ sound.

Sign **Ww**.

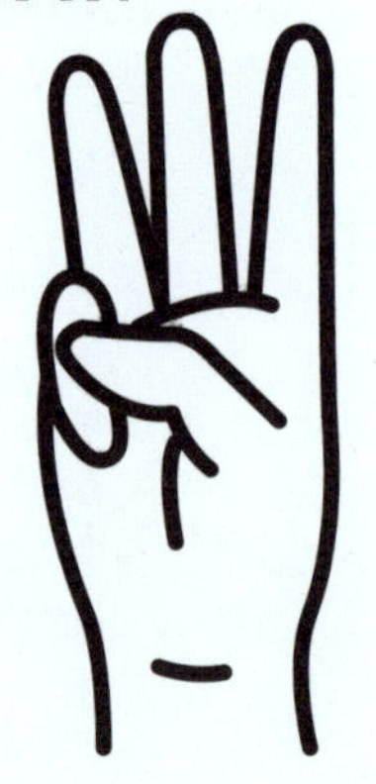

Say the name of each picture. What sound do you hear at the beginning?
Write **Ww** next to each picture.

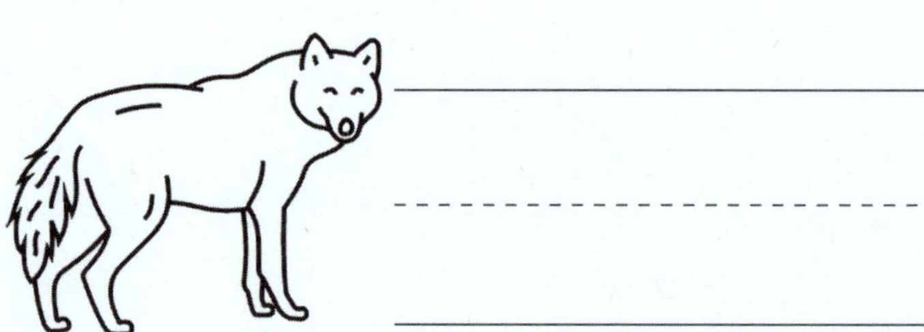

Trace the **W** and **w**'s.

Wolf saw a web.

Name: _______________________________ **Date:** _______________________

Say the name of each picture. Color four things that start with **W**.

Cut along the dashed lines. Weave the strip through the slots, as shown. Slide the strip to see the pictures and words.

fox

six

mix

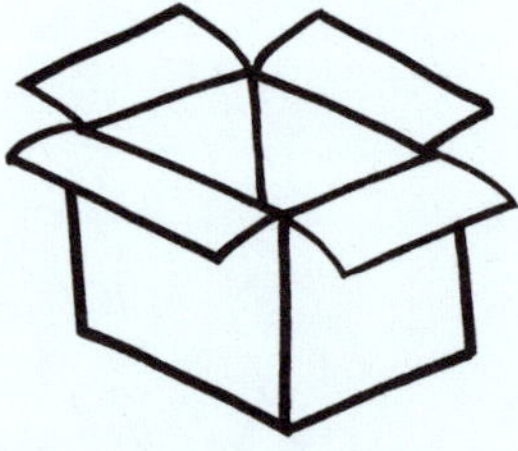
box

Name: _______________________   **Date:** _______________

Trace **Xx**. Say the /ks/ sound.

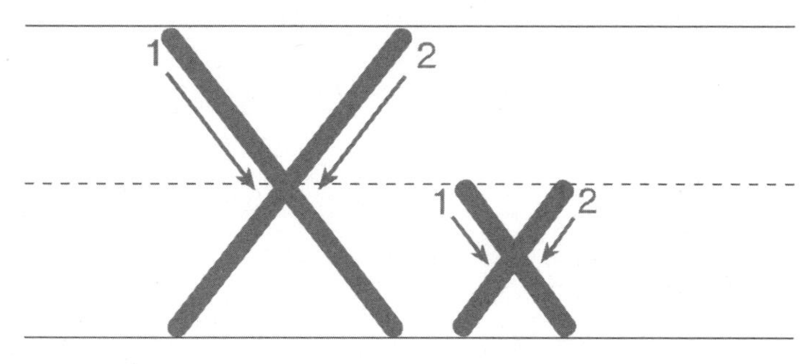

Sign **Xx**.

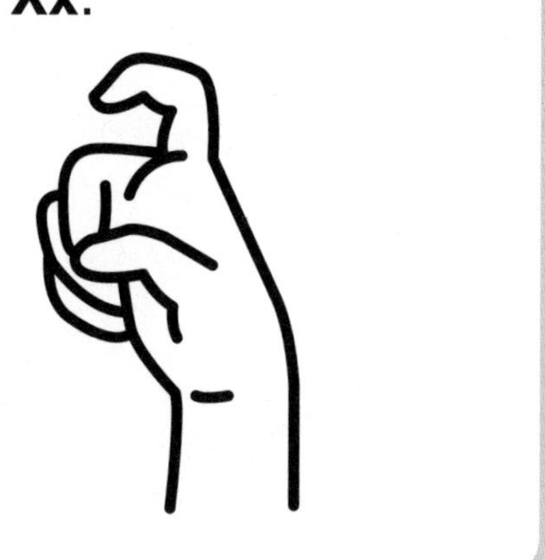

Say the name of each picture. What sound do you hear at the end?
Write **Xx** next to each picture.

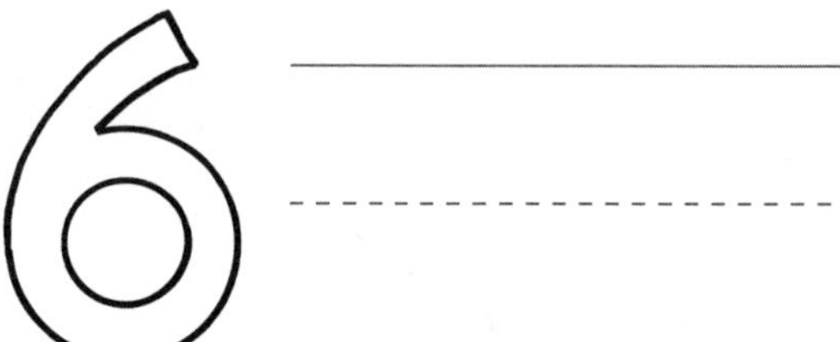

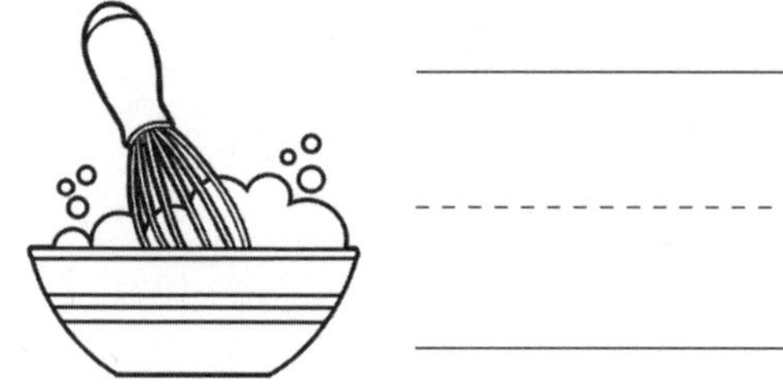

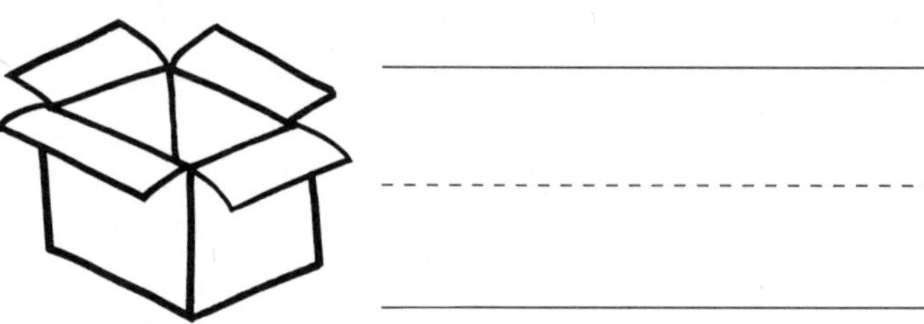

Trace the **x**'s.

Fox fixes six boxes.

Name: _______________________________ **Date:** _______________

Say the name of each picture. Color four things that end with **x**.

 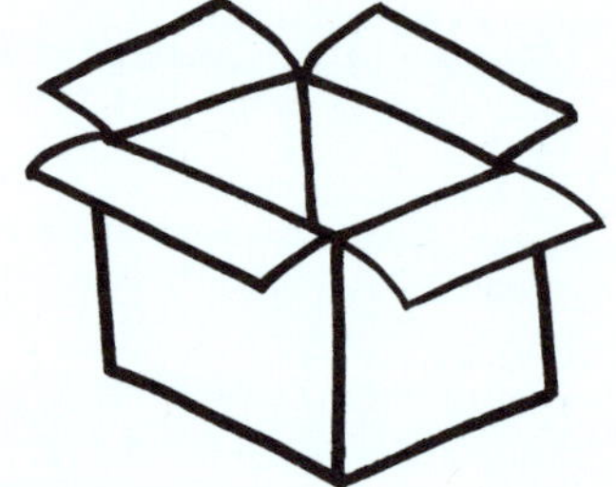 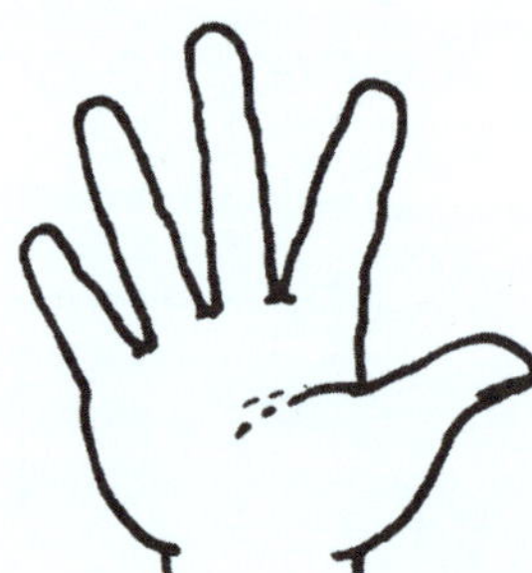

 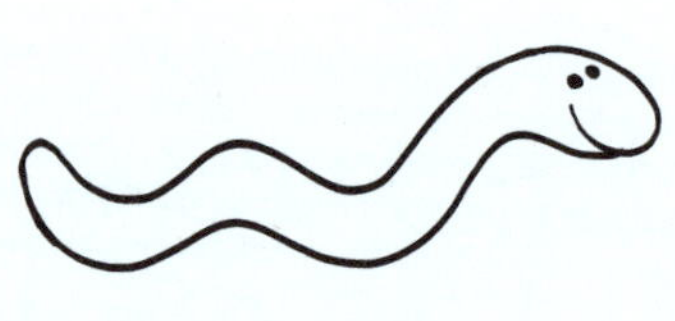 

Cut along the dashed lines. Weave the strip through the slots, as shown. Slide the strip to see the pictures and words.

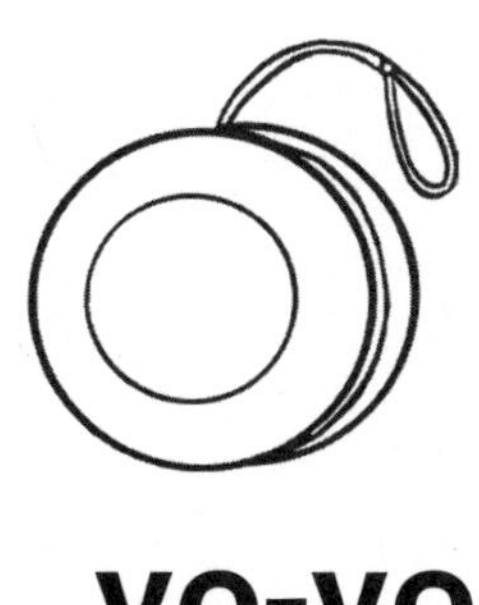

yo-yo

yarn

yogurt

yawn

Name: ____   **Date:** ______________

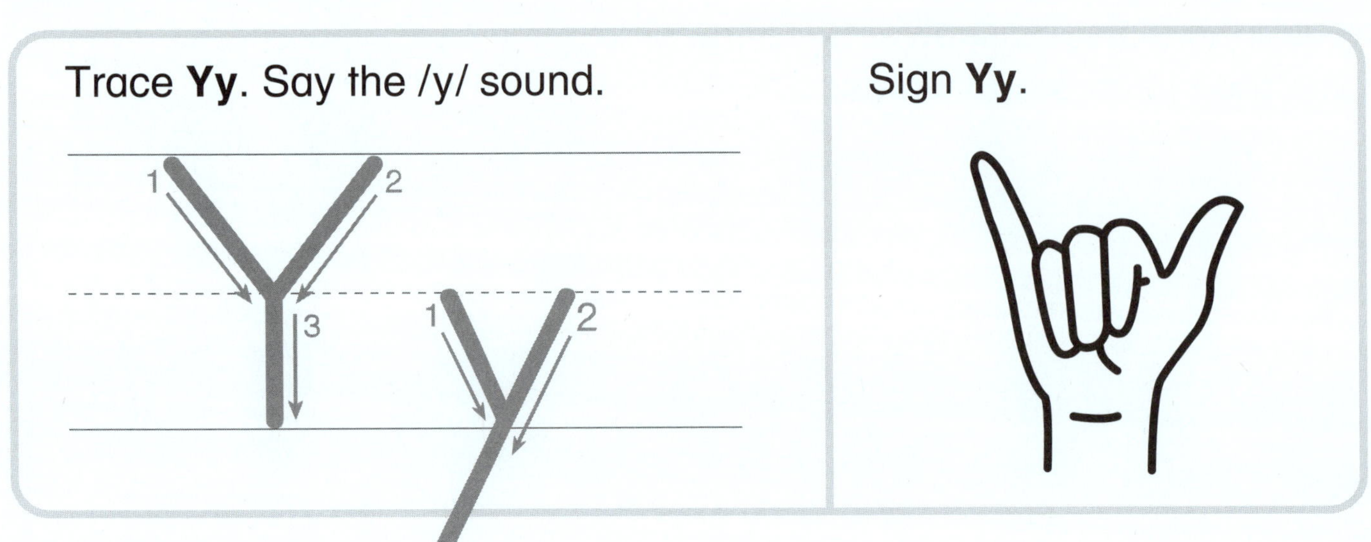

Trace **Yy**. Say the /y/ sound.

Sign **Yy**.

Say the name of each picture. What sound do you hear at the beginning? Write **Yy** next to each picture.

Trace the **Y** and **y**'s.

Name: ___________________________ **Date:** ___________________

Say the name of each picture. Color four things that start with **Y**.

Cut along the dashed lines. Weave the strip through the slots, as shown. Slide the strip to see the pictures and words.

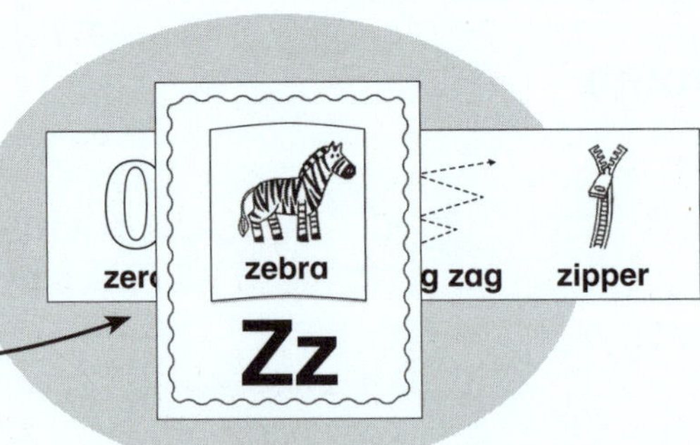

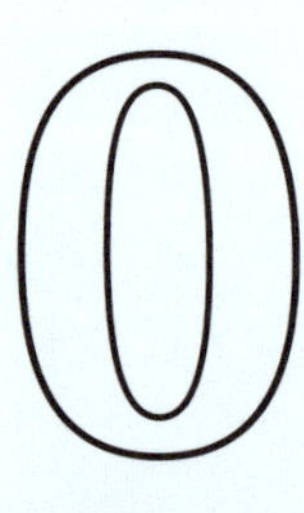
zero

zebra

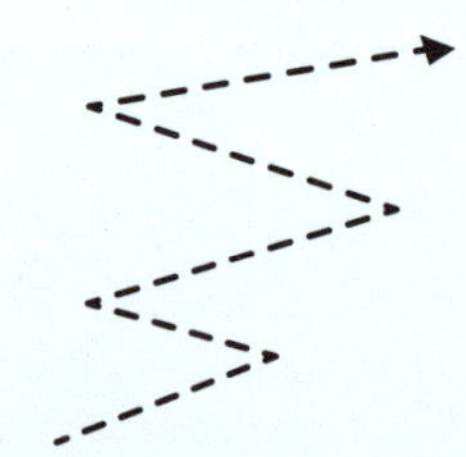
zig zag

zipper

Name: ___________________________   **Date:** ___________

Trace **Zz**. Say the /z/ sound.

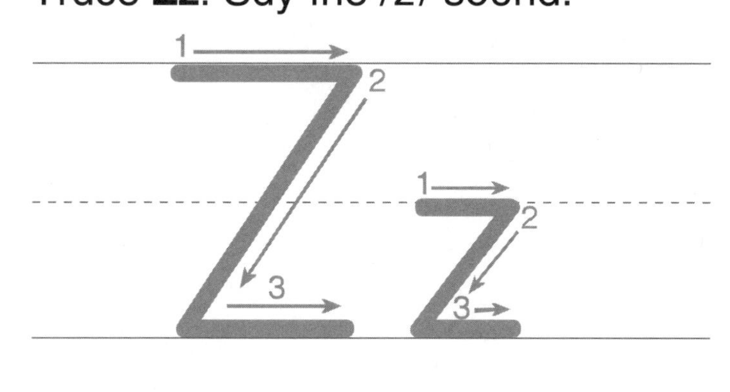

Sign **Zz**.

Say the name of each picture. What sound do you hear at the beginning? Write **Zz** next to each picture.

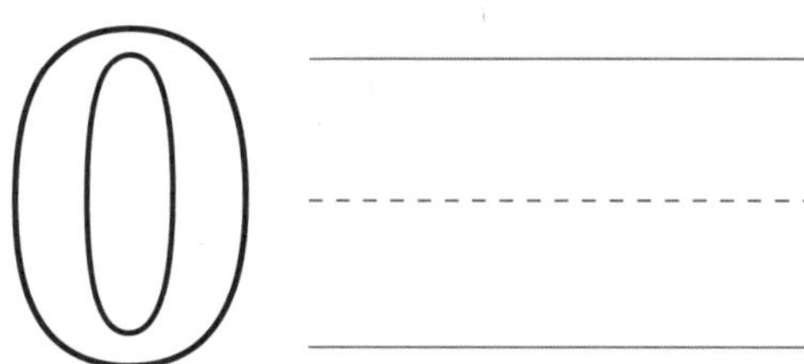

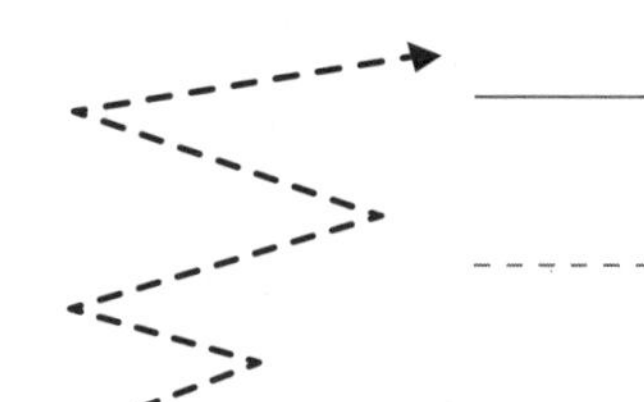

Trace the **Z** and **z**'s.

Zebra zips zippers.

Name: ___________________________ **Date:** _______________

Say the name of each picture. Color four things that start with **Z**.

Letter Flash Cards

Review letters and sounds with the set of reproducible flash cards on pages 87–93. The cards include upper- and lowercase letters, illustrations for each letter, and blank cards. You might want to photocopy cards on cardstock or laminate them for durability. Use the flash cards with the games and activities below to strengthen children's phonics skills and foster their excitement for learning. These activities are best used as a review after you have introduced the target letters.

Memory

Make pairs of cards using either the lower- or uppercase letter or a letter and the illustration that matches the beginning letter sound. (NOTE: The illustrations for the letter *x* match the ending sound instead.) Randomly arrange pairs of cards face down in a grid. Children take turns flipping any two cards. If the cards match, the child can keep them. If the cards do not match, the child returns the cards face down to their spots in the grid. The player with the most cards when all matches are made wins.

Alphabet Scavenger Hunt

Give each child an upper- or lowercase letter card. Invite children to walk around the room and find something that begins with their letter's sound. Instruct children to wait next to their found object until all players are ready. Children then take turns saying the letter on their card, the sound it makes, and the object they found.

Take-Home Mystery Letter Bag

Prepare the bag by placing a letter card and three to five blank cards inside the bag. Each week, invite a different child to take home the Mystery Letter Bag. Instruct the child to use the blank cards to draw (or write the names of) three to five objects they see at home that begin with the mystery letter. When the child returns with the Mystery Letter Bag, have them share their letter, the sound it makes, and the objects they found.

Three's Company

Create a bag containing one set of the three uppercase, lowercase, and illustration cards for each of the letters children have already learned. Ask children to sort the cards into their sets of three. Then invite them to say the letter sound of each set of cards.

Beginning Sounds Bingo

Make several copies of the picture cards for this small-group game. Give each child 16 picture cards and show them how to arrange the cards in a 4-by-4 grid. Once children are ready, call out a letter sound. Any child who has a picture in their grid that begins with that letter sound should turn that card face down. When a child has four face-down cards vertically, horizontally, or diagonally, that child calls out "Bingo!" and says the letter sounds that they have flipped to win. (NOTE: Do not use the letter *x* card for this activity.)

Alphabet Hopscotch

Create a hopscotch grid in your classroom using tape or take the learning outdoors using sidewalk chalk. Tape a letter card face up inside each square of the grid. As children hop in each square, they should say the letter name or the letter sound on the card.

ABC Order

Give children bags containing one lowercase or uppercase letter card for each of the letters they have learned. Instruct children to arrange the cards alphabetically. If needed, provide an alphabet chart for children's reference.

Tag Team

Using pairs of upper- and lowercase letter flash cards, distribute one card to each child. Invite children to move about the room, saying the sound of the letter they are holding, to find the classmate with the letter that matches theirs. As an alternative, use pairs of one letter card and its picture card, or use all three cards in each set to create groups of three children.

I Spy

Give pairs of children a bag containing the letter cards. One child draws a letter card from the bag, then looks around the room for an object that begins with that letter. The player says, "I spy something that begins with the letter _." Player Two tries to guess the object. Once they have guessed correctly, Player Two draws a new letter and chooses an object for Player One to guess. (NOTE: Do not use the letter *x* card for this activity.)

Head, Shoulders, Knees, and Toes

Hold up a letter flash card. Invite children to put their hands on their heads as they say the name of the letter, then touch their shoulders as they say the letter sound, touch their knees as they say a word that begins with that letter sound, and finally, touch their toes as they repeat the name of the letter. (For example, "A, /a/, apple, A.")

Letter and Picture Flash Cards

A	a	
B	b	
C	c	
D	d	

E	e	
F	f	
G	g	
H	h	

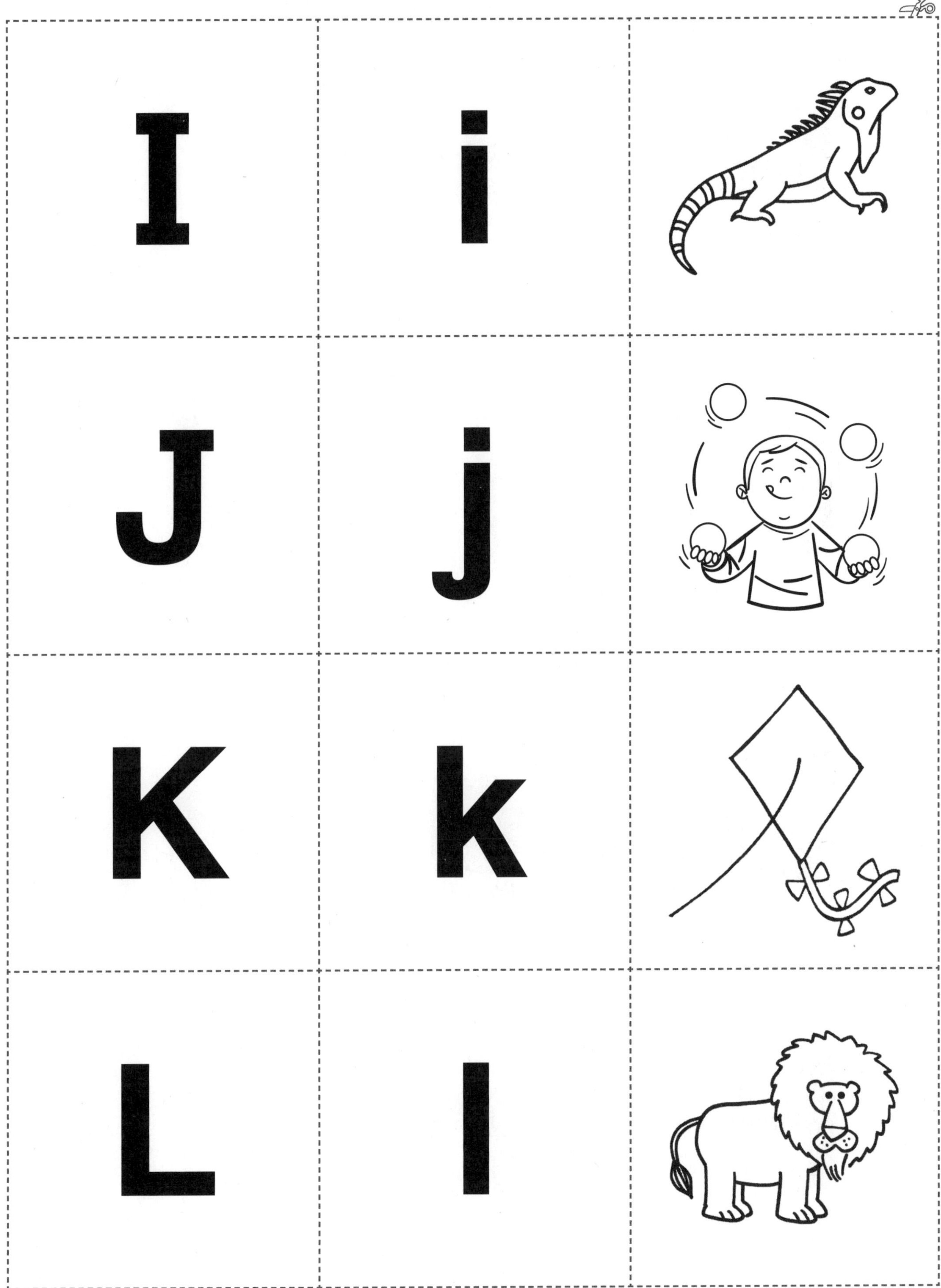

I i
J j
K k
L l

<table>
<tr><td>M</td><td>m</td><td></td></tr>
<tr><td>N</td><td>n</td><td>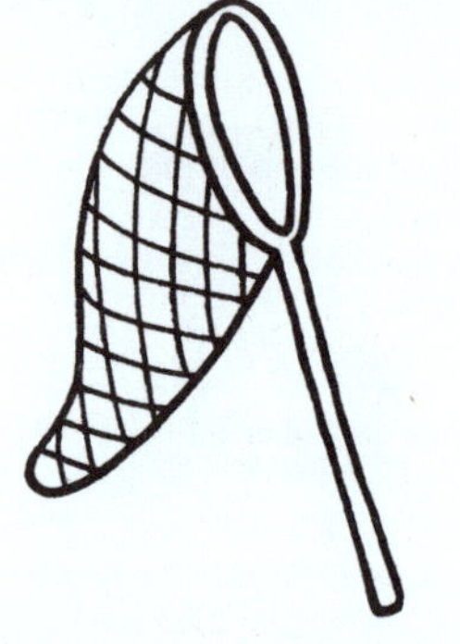</td></tr>
<tr><td>O</td><td>o</td><td></td></tr>
<tr><td>P</td><td>p</td><td></td></tr>
</table>

Q	q	
R	r	
S	s	
T	t	

U u
V v
W W
X x

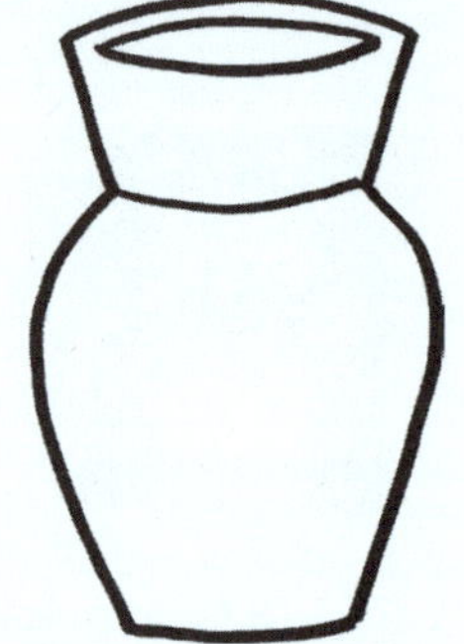

Y

y

Z

z

Answer Key

Letter *Aa* (page 9)

Letter *Dd* (page 18)

Letter *Gg* (page 27)

Letter *Bb* (page 12)

Letter *Ee* (page 21)

Letter *Hh* (page 30)

Letter *Cc* (page 15)

Letter *Ff* (page 24)

Letter *Ii* (page 33)

Answer Key

Letter *Jj* (page 36)

Letter *Mm* (page 45)

Letter *Pp* (page 54)

Letter *Kk* (page 39)

Letter *Nn* (page 48)

Letter *Qq* (page 57)

Letter *Ll* (page 42)

Letter *Oo* (page 51)

Letter *Rr* (page 60)

Answer Key

Letter *Ss* (page 63)

Letter *Vv* (page 72)

Letter *Yy* (page 81)

Letter *Tt* (page 66)

Letter *Ww* (page 75)

Letter *Zz* (page 84)

Letter *Uu* (page 69)

Letter *Xx* (page 78)